ICELANDIC WHALES

PAST AND PRESENT

*Sigurður Ægisson, Jón Ásgeir í Aðaldal,
Jón Baldur Hlíðberg*

Preface by Mark Carwardine

English translation by Daniel Teague

FORLAGIÐ

table
of contents

Icelandic whales, past and present
© Jón Ásgeir í Aðaldal, Sigurður Ægisson,
Jón Baldur Hlíðberg, 1997
English translation: Daniel Teague
Prentsmiðjan Oddi hf.
Printed in Iceland
FORLAGIÐ • Reykjavík • 1997

preface
Mark Carwardine

It was nearly one o'clock in the morning and the calm sea was bathed in a soft, golden glow from the midnight sun. We were gathered on the deck of an elegant wooden fishing boat, in a protected bay off the north-eastern coast of Iceland, gazing at the scene before us in stunned silence. There were five minke whales around the boat, their dark bodies sending golden ripples across the glassy surface of the sea and their blows producing colourful displays of droplets in the rays of the sun. Meanwhile, hundreds of arctic terns were wheeling and diving almost within arm's reach of where we were standing. It was a night that none of us will ever forget.

Whale watching was unknown in Iceland before the 1990s. But in the space of just a few years it has become a major attraction for nature travellers from all over the world. Suddenly, there are whale-watching ports in Húsavík, Höfn, Grindavík, Keflavík, Búðir, Arnarstapi, Ólafsvík, Hauganes and Dalvík, and no doubt there will be even more in the years to come.

I have been fortunate to watch whales in many parts of the world, but I can honestly say that Iceland will always remain a firm favourite. Where else can you encounter minke whales in the light of the midnight sun? Or watch humpback whales against a spectacular backdrop of active volcanoes and snow-capped mountains? Where else in Europe can you find blue whales with such regularity? Or have a good chance of encountering fin whales, sperm whales, orcas, Atlantic white-sided

dolphins, white-beaked dolphins and harbour porpoises? With so many different species, and such a deep-seated knowledge of the sea, perhaps it is not surprising that Iceland is rapidly becoming a world leader in this specialised field.

I have been visiting Iceland several times a year for more than fifteen years, and now it feels like a second home. It is a wonderful country that exerts a powerful hold over many of its visitors. The fact that it is now a major whale watching destination, as well, seems almost too good to be true.

Therefore it gives me great pleasure to recommend this delightful book. Sigurður, Jón Ásgeir and Jón Baldur have produced an invaluable guide which I am sure will inspire a great many people to get out and meet for themselves the exotic, mysterious and graceful denizens of the sea, the whales. There are never any guarantees, of course, but that is the nature of wildlife watching. Just book one of the many trips on offer around the country, keep your fingers crossed, and you will not be disappointed. I can guarantee that a close encounter with one of these magnificent creatures will be the highlight of your holiday.

Good luck!

March 1997, Mark Carwardine

origin
of whales

People have found it difficult to determine the origin of whales since the question is complex. Palaeontology is a relatively young discipline; thus, what is known today, generally speaking, may be obsolete tomorrow. Still, most people today favour the view that whales (*Cetacea*) have developed from primitive land animals of the order of *Condylarthra*, belonging to the *Mesonychida* family that existed about 55 million years ago. These animals' appearance was similar to a wolf's. Their size was between that of a modern dog and a bear. However, precisely which species was involved is difficult to say because, so far, no direct link from such an animal to whales has been found. Experts believe that one of the smaller species is most likely, and that the adaptation from dwelling on land to life in the sea first occurred somewhere near where Pakistan is today, in the eastern part of the Tethys. One day, then, the predecessor of whales began to search for food in the shallows there and gradually began to spend more time in the sea than on land, undergoing the relevant physical changes. The disappearance of dinosaurs, 10 million years before, left a certain vacuum in nature, which, along with various geographical changes occurring about this time, created the conditions favouring this new form of life.

The next step in the whale's development can be seen in an animal relatively recently discovered in 50- to 53-million-year-old sedimentary layers in Pakistan. Its scientific name is *Pakicetus*. It is the most primitive type of whale known.

About 50 million years ago, *Protocetus* made its appearance. Its fossilised bones were discovered in the El Fajúm-depression in Egypt.

Protocetus, because it still

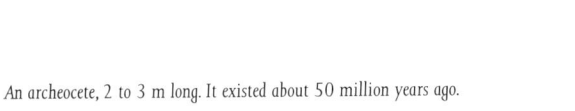

An archeocete, 2 to 3 m long. It existed about 50 million years ago.

had a pelvis, was unlike contemporary whales. In addition, its shape more resembled that of a giant snake or eel. Its length was two to three metres. Similar remains were also found in India and surrounding areas.

Then, in sedimentary layers in North America, New Zealand and the South Pole, dating to 45 million years ago, a whale was found that in Icelandic is called "saw-tooth" (*Basilosaurus* or *Zeuglodon*). It was also an ancient whale (archeocete) like *Protocetus* and *Pakicetus*.

Whales, like men, have evolved from animals something like this one, an insectivore, which existed in the time of the dinosaurs.

The first *basilosaurus* fossil was dug up in 1832 in the state of Louisiana in the United States. The animal is believed to have been about 15 or 20 m long, weighing some five tons. The pelvis, found in the above archeocetes, had disappeared along with almost all trace of rear legs. The shape of the whale's body, however, was like its predecessors', long and slender and nearly hairless. This showed a great leap forward. The dorsal fin had developed and very likely some form of flukes. For some reason, this species died out about 38 million years ago.

Contemporary whales, both toothed and baleen whales, are believed to have developed some 30 to 40 million years ago from some of the *basilosaurus* predecessors.

An animal that could be a link between the archeocetes and baleen whales was discovered in sedimentary layers in Australia, dating to 24 million years ago. Called *Mammalodon*, it had teeth of a very peculiar sort. Where they came together from the upper and lower gums, they formed a sort of filter. The flukes resembled those of the beaked whales (one of the families of toothed whales), but the *Mammalodon* had throat grooves.

history
of whale studies

The oldest, preserved remains concerning encounters between men and whales are found in Norway, 9,000 to 10,000 years old, and in Alaska, 5,000 or 6,000 years old (perhaps even 8,000 years old). World literature also has many early references to these mysterious beasts, both in religious and secular writings. For example, the story of the creation in Genesis in the Old Testament tells of when God created the large animals of the sea. There is also the well-known Old Testament account of Jonah who ended up in a whale's belly and, after three days, was returned to land. The story is believed to have been written in the fourth century BC. There are also various references in Greek

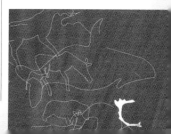

In Dyreberget at Leiknes in Tysfjord in North-Norway, which was "discovered" in 1915, there are to be found the oldest preserved relics of encounters between whales and men. These are various animal drawings engraved on cliffs in the open air. The picture shows one of them, a 7.63 m long killer whale. The engraving is considered to be 9–10 thousand years old and is among the largest found in Europe.

Jonah and the whale from the account in the Old Testament (Jonah 2: 1-11). An old dry point on copper by Joan Sadler.

works, for example, the zoology of the philosopher and biologist Aristotle (384-322 BC), from a period similar to that of the tale of Jonah, where he gives an exhaustive, scientific account of over 500 species, discussing, among other things, marine mammals. Scholars conclude that he had, in all likelihood, become acquainted with marine mammals from his own experience with the sea surrounding the Greek island of Lesbos off the coast of Turkey where he lived. Aristotle's description of dolphins is so precise that contemporary scientists believe they can add little to it. In fact, few developments occurred in this area until about 1500 years later, and then here in the North Atlantic. The Norwegian treatise Speculum regale, or The King's Mirror, was written in the 13th century, probably for the sons of Hakon, the Old, King of Norway. It contains moral teachings in addition to various lore about geography, sailing, warfare, etc. One part of it states: "In the oceans off Iceland, little seems to me worth remembering or discussing except the whales there in the waters, which are quite various…"

Mass on the Open Sea. The story of the Irish Saint Bréanainn (in Latin, Brendanus; in English and many other languages, Brendan. Lived in the 6th century.) who sang Easter Mass on the back of a giant whale that rose from the ocean at the Almighty's behest. The tale was first written in Navigatio Sancti Brendani from the 9th or 10th century, which recounts various fantastic stories of his sea voyages. The document is thought to be based on older narratives, on the one hand, about the Irish seafarer, Manannán Mac Lir, and on the other hand, about the Irish champion, Maol Dúin. The roots, tales of an enormous whale that is mistaken for an island in the open ocean, reach much farther back in time. This stylised account of the event first appeared in the manuscript Nova Typis Transacta Navigato, in 1621.

Following these words is a detailed section about whale species off the country's coasts. This was the best, most precise material written up to then and would also serve as a basic reference on this topic for a long time. Then, in 1640, Jón Gudmundsson the Learned wrote On Iceland's Diverse Nature.

The King's Mirror originally had pictures of whales, but they have perished over time.

The Book of Settlement (Landnámabók) and 17 of the Icelandic sagas mention whales in one way or another. However, it is seldom possible to determine what kind of whale is involved. When a whale stranded, ownership disputes sometimes arose concerning the animal, and on occasion, they ended in slayings. Very early on, therefore, people considered it necessary to enact laws and regulations concerning these things. This can be seen in the country's old lawbooks as well as in the Collection of Icelandic Ancient Letters.

Some of the names of whales, such as "redcombe", "horse whale", "cirriped", etc., are quite exotic to contemporary readers, and it is thus nearly impossible to guess exactly the whale species that are being reported, although

Whale cutting. Picture from one of the 14th century manuscripts of Jónsbók. In previous centuries, whale strandings were considered a great find and domestic boon. They often saved whole regions where people were starving. Some even think that these animals were the chief source of meat for people in Iceland during the Saga Age and long after that. Nowadays, if a whale strands on a beach, people are not as happy as they were centuries ago. However, traces of the old days still survive in the Icelandic language, where "whale stranding" is a common metaphor for a great stroke of luck.

This part of the Bishop in Hólar, Gudbrandur Thorláksson's Map of Iceland, ca. 1590, clearly shows the ideas people had about whales in the ocean around Iceland at that time. Many stories from the 17th, 18th and 19th centuries and even in the 20th century contain descriptions of fantastic creatures that followed boats on the open ocean and tried to destroy them.

many people have tried. In the treatise of Jón the Learned, there are several pictures, but although he uses many of the same names as are in the old Norwegian treatise, the considerable gap between the 13th and 17th centuries makes it inconclusive whether the same species are involved. But that is the way of things. Snorri Björnsson of Húsafell (1710-1803) later added to this work of Jón the Learned. After this, developments in whale studies were few until the Swede, Carl von Linné (1707-1778), otherwise known as Linnaeus, came

along. After him, one marine biologist after another appeared, Frenchmen, Germans, Dutchmen and Britons being the most prominent. Later on, there were Americans, Danes and Belgians. Systematic research on whales near and around Iceland, however, did not begin until about 1965, and Norway and England played a special part in this.

Experts generally deem there to be 78 contemporary species of whale. Some, however, say

The picture shows part of one principal manuscript of the The King's Mirror, the Norwegian parchment, which is thought to have been written in 1275, or thereabouts.

Red combe is first mentioned in Grágás, an old Icelandic lawbook. The next reference to these whales occurs in The King's Mirror from the 13th century, where they are said to be full of greediness and wickedness. The King's Mirror originally included pictures of these whales and others, but they where lost over time. This picture, taken from the treatise of Jón Gudmundsson, the Learned, shows a red combe. Gudmundsson's sources for their appearance are not clear.

there are more, up to 90 species. This difference stems from how some of the known whales are classified. The question, in other words, is whether, for example, the right whale should be regarded as one species or three, etc. Regardless of how this is resolved, it is just as probable that more whale species than the above figures indicate lurk in the ocean depths (the greatest part of which are unexplored and cover 70% of the earth's surface). A supporting example is that some whale species are known only from a few strandings of individual whales, and, in some cases, there are only eyewitness accounts to go by. This is especially pertinent to one genus of beaked whales (*Ziphiidae*), called *Mesoplodon*. Most of them, nine species in all, were not discovered until the first part of this century. One was not given an official name until 1991; this was the lesser beaked whale (*Mesoplodon peruvianus*), the smallest member of the family.

whales
Today

On the basis of the knowledge now available and the findings of palaeontology, the order of whales (*Cetacea*) is generally divided into three suborders: a) ancient whales (*Archaeoceti*), b) baleen whales (*Mysticeti*) and c) toothed whales (*Odontoceti*).

The ancient whales, which are all extinct, were a certain type of toothed whale. Toothed whales include 68 extant species, and baleen whales 10 species, if the total figure assumed is 78. The most numerous family of toothed whales is *Delphinidae* (the blackfish, including: the white-beaked dolphin, the long-finned pilot whale, the killer whale, Atlantic white-sided dolphin, the common dolphin, striped dolphin, bottlenose dolphin, etc.) with 31 species. Next, comes *Ziphiidae* (beaked whales, for example, the northern bottlenose whale, Cuvier's beaked whale and the *Mesoplodon*) with 20 species. Then, there are the *Phocoenidae* (porpoises) with six species, the *Platanistidae* (river dolphins) with five species, the *Monodontidae* (narwhal and beluga whales) with three species, the *Kogiidae* (pygmy and dwarf sperm whales) with two species and, finally, the *Physeteridae* (the sperm whale) with one species.

The most numerous family of baleen whales is *Balaenopteridae* (the rorquals) with six species, then the *Balaenidae* (the bowhead whale, the right whale) with two species and *Neobalaenidae* (pygmy right whale) and *Eschrichtiidae* (Gray whale), bringing up the rear, each with only one species.

There is a considerable difference between the two contemporary suborders of whale, *Odontoceti* and *Mysticeti*, especially with regard to the following: a) The species of *Odontoceti* have symmetrical skulls, while those of the species of *Mysticeti* are asymmetrical. b) The species of *Odontoceti* employ a kind of sonar technology, in addition to sight and hearing, for their hunting. Some can even cripple their prey with bursts of high-frequency sound. Most species of *Mysticeti* have to make do with more primitive methods, based on sight, etc. c) All species of *Odontoceti* are toothed (to some extent), but the species of *Mysticeti* have instead a kind of filtration equipment (horny plates and/or great stiff hairs) called baleens. d) The species of *Odontoceti* have only one nostril or blowhole (the other one is "plugged"), while the species of *Mysticeti* have two. e) The male *Odontoceti*, nearly without exception, are larger than the females, but this is reversed for the species of *Mysticeti*. f)

The pregnancies of female *Odontoceti* generally are longer and less frequent than for female *Mysticeti*. g) The species of *Odontoceti* are, on average, much more gregarious than those of *Mysticeti*.

Experts generally agree that 23 species of whale have been seen off the coasts of Iceland, that is, 15 toothed whale species and eight baleen whale species. The toothed whale species, in alphabetical order, are the following: Atlantic white-sided dolphin, beluga whale, Blainville's beaked whale, bottlenose dolphin, common dolphin, Cuvier's beaked whale, harbour porpoise, killer whale, long-finned pilot whale, narwhal, northern bottlenose whale, sperm whale, striped dolphin, white-beaked dolphin. The baleen whales are the blue whale, bowhead whale, Gray whale, humpback whale, minke whale, fin whale, right whale and sei whale.

It is generally agreed that there are 78 known species of whale in the world. However, this does not mean that somewhere in the depths of the ocean, which covers more than 70% of the earth's surface, more species are not lurking, waiting to be discovered. One of them could, for example, be this animal, whose picture is based on descriptions of 33 eyewitnesses in many parts of the world. The creature's name is Many-humped sea serpent. In many respects, it resembles whales, for example, the black colour on its back and its white underbelly, dorsal fin and flukes. The picture is taken from the French-Belgian naturalist Bernhard Heuvelman's book "Le Grand Serpent-de-mer", published in 1965 and has since been regarded as the chief treatise of those who believe that there are more animals on earth, in the air and in the sea, than science has discovered. The Many-humped creature has twice been spotted east of Iceland.

Toothed whales' ages can be calculated in a manner similar to the way a tree's age is calculated. The growth of a longitudinally cut tooth is inspected. The growths are like the annual rings of tree trunks. One light ring and one dark correspond to a year in a whale's life.

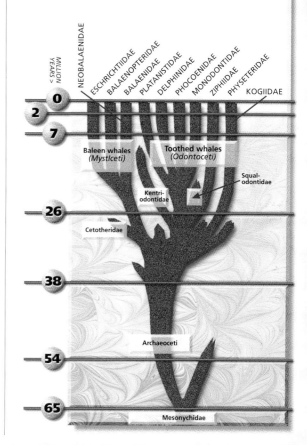

BELUGA WHALE / *Delphinapterus leucas*

Distribution

id checklist

BODY: Thick, resembles a torpedo. Light-yellow or completely white (fully grown animals); calves very dark (grey or brownish), lightening with age. Small, domed head. Abrupt snout. Neck vertebrae not fused; can turn head in all directions and change shape of mouth and lips.

DORSAL FIN: None. A small ridge or upright band in the middle of the back.

FLIPPERS: Spatulate, relatively broad and short, slightly arched; very movable.

FLUKES: Often dark-brown on the back edge; notched in middle. Rounded ends.

DIVING: Usually close to the surface, shallow dives for short periods (1 to 2 minutes).

BLOWING: Low, but audible at several hundred metres in favourable weather.

SWIMMING: Usually swims slowly; believed capable of swimming backward at low speed.

HABITAT: Often near the coast and even in shallows. Primarily a cold-sea whale, although it does not frequent deep waters. Known to swim up large rivers in colder countries, looking for salmon, often going far upriver (up to 1,000 km).

NATURE: Tame and, therefore, relatively easy to approach. Often spy-hops. Known for making many beautiful high-frequency sounds. Never breaches.

Order:	Whales (*Cetacea*), 78 species.
Suborder:	Toothed whales (*Odontoceti*), 68 species.
Superfamily:	Dolphins (*Delphinoidea*), 40 species.
Family:	White whales (*Monodontidae*), 3 species.
Subfamily:	Delphinapterinae, 3 species.
Genus:	*Delphinapterus*, 1 species.
Species:	*D. leucas*.

Length/weight (newborn):	1.5-1.6 m / 80 kg.
Length (adult):	♀ 3-4.1 m. ♂ 4.2-5.5 m.
Weight (adult):	♀ 400-600 kg. ♂ 1-1.6 tons.
Lifetime:	30 years, maybe 40.
World population:	50,000-70,000.
In Icelandic waters:	An occasional guest.
Group size:	(1-4) 5-20(1,000+).
Diet:	

Delphinapterus leucas (Pallas, 1776).
Synonym: *Balaena albicans, Beluga angustata, Beluga borealis, Beluga canadensis, Beluga catodon, Beluga concreta, Beluga declivis, Beluga glacialis, Beluga kingi, Beluga leucas, Beluga rhinodon, Catodon albicans, Catodon candicans, Catodon sibbaldi, Delphinapterus beluga, Delphinapterus catodon, Delphinapterus dorofeevi, Delphinapterus freimani, Delphinapterus kingi, Delphinapterus kingii, Delphinapterus leucas dorofeevi, Delphinapterus leucas marisalbi, Delphinus albians, Delphinus albicans, Delphinus canadensis, Delphinus kingii, Delphinus leucas, Delphinus leucaster, Inia canadensis, Physeter katadon, Physeter macrocephalus albicans, Selphinus phocaena albus.*

Mjaldur. Mjallur; hvitfiskur; HVÍTHVALUR; hvitingur.

Kvitkval. Beluga; kvitfisk.

Beluga. Ballena blanca.

Beluga. Delfinattero bianco.

Weißwal. Belucha; Beluga; Weißfisch.

Bélouga. Baleine blanche; beluga; béluga; béluga vrai; dauphin blanc; delphinaptère blanc; marsouin blanc; moine de mer.

Beluga whale. Beluga; belukha; northern beluga; sea-canary; sea canary; small catodon; white fish; white porpoise; white whale.

Delphinapterus is a compound of the Greek words *delphin* (= dolphin), *a* (= without) and *pteron* (= wing, that is, horn). *Leucas* is derived from the Greek word *leukos* (= white); *the white dolphin without a dorsal fin.*

beluga whale
Delphinapterus leucas

BODY: Thick, resembles a torpedo. Males (and usually only males) have a long tusk (up to 2.7 m). Coloration varies by age. The calves are born brown, dark-grey or bluish, later darkening to black in adolescence. When approaching sexual maturity, however, the animals begin to lighten in colour, first on the underbelly. Then, they take on a dappled or mottled pattern unique among whales. The dark colour also becomes greenish. Very old animals become almost completely white, especially males. The head is small and domed; the snout is hardly discernible and the mouth small.

DORSAL FIN: None.

FLIPPERS: Relatively broad and short; with age, the ends turn up slightly.

FLUKES: Most resemble a fan gathered in the middle.

DIVING: Generally submerge for 7 to 20 minutes; common for all animals in pod to dive at same time.

BLOWING: Weak and indistinct.

SWIMMING: Swims slowly while hunting; otherwise travels relatively fast.

HABITAT: A whale of the shallows, choosing to stay somewhat offshore. Primarily a cold-water whale, staying close to the polar ice.

NATURE: Lively on surface, although generally does not breach.

MORE INFORMATION ON PAGE 57

Order:	Whales (Cetacea), 78 species.
Suborder:	Toothed whales (Odontoceti), 68 species.
Superfamily:	Dolphins (Delphinoidea), 40 species.
Family:	White whales (Monodontidae), 3 species.
Subfamily:	Monodontinae, 1 species.
Genus:	Monodon, 1 species.
Species.:	M. monoceros.

A narwhal from the treatise of Jón Gudmundsson the Learned from 1640.

Length/weight (newborn):	1.5-1.7 m / 80 kg.	
Length (adult):	♀ 3.5-5.1 m.	♂ 4.1-6.2 m.
Weight (adult):	♀ 800 kg-1.3 tn.	♂ 1.2-1.6 tons.
Lifetime:	50 years.	
World population:	25,000-50,000.	
In Icelandic waters:	An occasional guest.	
Group size:	(1-2) 3-20(1,000+).	
Diet:		

Monodon monoceros (Linnaeus, 1758).
Synonym: *Ceratodon monodon, Monodon marinum, Monodon narhval, Monodon narwal, Narwalus andersonianus, Narwalus microcephalus, Narwalus vulgaris, Tachynices megacephalus, Unicornu marinum.*

 Náhvalur. NÁHVELI.

 Narkval. Hornfisk.

 Narval.

 Narvalo.

 Narwal. Einhorn; Einhornwal; See-Einhorn.

 Narval. Licorne de mer; monodon; narval monocéros; Unicorne.

 Narwhale. Narwal; narwhal; sea-unicorn; sea unicorn; unicorn; unicorn whale.

Monodon is a compound of the Greek words *monos* (= alone; individual) and *odon* (= tooth). *Monoceros* is a compound of the Greek words *monos* (= alone; individual) and *keros* (= horn); *the one-toothed whale; unicorn.*

narwhal
Monodon monoceros

Distribution

HARBOUR PORPOISE / *Phocoena phocoena*

id
checklist

BODY: Thick and short but very rakish build; generally dark-grey on top, but lighter colour on sides and underbelly. Head small and rounded. Low forehead, abrupt snout. Tail stock very thin and weak in appearance, compared with other porpoises.

DORSAL FIN: Rather low and triangular.

FLIPPERS: Small and dark-grey.

FLUKES: Small.

DIVING: Usually dives for 2 to 6 minutes at a time.

BLOWING: Not discernible, but sometimes quite audible.

SWIMMING: Often lies motionless on surface for long periods. Otherwise, swims relatively slowly, but can, if pursuing fast-swimming prey, surge over the surface of the water.

HABITAT: Exclusively a shallow-water whale, hunting food along the ocean bottom; preferred depth 10 to 100 (1,000) m.

NATURE: Little interest in boats; seldom breaches.

Order:	Whales (*Cetacea*), 78 species.
Suborder:	Toothed whales (*Odontoceti*), 68 species.
Superfamily:	Dolphins (*Delphinoidea*), 40 species.
Family:	Phocoenidae, 6 species.
Subfamily:	Phocoeninae, 4 species.
Genus:	*Phocoena*, 4 species.
Species:	*P. phocoena*.

Length/weight (newborn):	0.67-0.85 m / 5 kg.
Length (adult):	♀ 1.4-1.89 m. ♂ 1.9 m.
Weight (adult):	♀ 55-60 kg. ♂ 70 kg.
Lifetime:	30 years.
World population:	Unknown.
In Icelandic waters:	Unknown.
Group size:	1, 2-10(250+).
Diet:	(fish (squid fish))

Phocoena phocoena (Linnaeus, 1758).
Synonym: *Delphinus phocaena, Delphinus phocaena phocaena, Delphinus ventricosus, Phocaena americana, Phocaena brachium, Phocaena brachycium, Phocaena communis, Phocaena lineata, Phocaena phocaena, Phocaena phocaena acuminata, Phocaena phocaena relicta, Phocaena phocaena vomerina, Phocaena phocoena acuminata conidens, Phocaena relicta, Phocaena rondeletii, Phocaena tuberculifera, Phocaena vomerina, Phocena phocoena, Phocoena vomerina.*

 Selhnísa. HNÍSA; hvalhnísa; höfrungshnísa.

 Nise.

 Marsopa común. Arroaz; cochino de mar; focena; fouliña; golfin; golfiño; marsopa; marsopa atlántica; marsopla; porco de mar; puerco de mar; puerco marino; tonina.

 Focena comune. Focena; marsovino; marsuino.

 Schweinswal. Braunfisch; Gemeiner Braunfisch; Kleiner Tümmler; Meerschwein; Schweinwal; Tümmler.

 Marsouin. Cochon de mer; marsouin commun; marsouin franc; poursille.

 Harbour porpoise. Atlantic harbor porpoise; common porpoise; harbor porpoise; herring hog; hog-fish; morhock; nisack; Pacific harbor porpoise; pellick; pelloch; perkin; porkpisce; porpesse; porpice; porpoise; porpus; puffing pig; sea-hog; sniffer.

Phocoena is believed to be derived either from the Greek word *phokaina* (= porpoise), which is derived from *phoke* (= seal), or the Latin word *phoca* (= seal); **the seal whale** (that is, the little whale resembling a seal).

harbour porpoise
Phocoena phocoena

MORE INFORMATION ON PAGE 61

id checklist

BODY: White, gray and black; complex pattern, not always clearly defined. White stripe along side. Nose often very light-coloured. Pale grey patch on side of tail stock.

DORSAL FIN: Prominent. Curves slightly backward at top; situated centrally; dark-coloured.

FLIPPERS: Rather long and broad, tapering sharply at ends; dark-coloured.

FLUKES: Notched in middle; sharply pointed ends.

DIVING: Generally stays close to surface.

BLOWING: Not visible.

SWIMMING: Moves fast and decisively.

HABITAT: Sometimes in shallows, but is mainly in open ocean; preferred depth is 100 to 1,000 m.

NATURE: Can be playful. Eagerly follows ships and boats, but gets bored quickly.

Order:	Whales (*Cetacea*), 78 species.
Suborder:	Toothed whales (*Odontoceti*), 68 species.
Superfamily:	Dolphins (*Delphinoidea*), 40 species.
Family:	*Delphinidae*, 31 species.
Subfamily:	*Delphininae*, 14 species.
Genus:	*Lagenorhynchus*, 6 species.
Species:	*L. albirostris*.

Length/weight (newborn):	1.2-1.6 m / 40 kg.
Length (adult):	♀ 2.5-3.05 m. ♂ 3.15 m.
Weight (adult):	♀ 180-250 kg. ♂ 250-370 kg.
Lifetime:	20-30 years, maybe 40.
World population:	Unknown.
In Icelandic waters:	12,000-20,000.
Group size:	(1) 10-100(1,000+).
Diet:	

Lagenorhynchus albirostris (Gray, 1846).
Synonym: *Delphinus albirostris, Delphinus ibseni, Delphinus pseudotursio, Delphinus tursio.*

 Blettahnýðir. HNÍÐINGUR; höfrungur.

 Kvitnos. Springer.

 Delfín de hocico blanco. Lagenorrinco; tursio; tursión.

 Lagenorinco rostrobianco. Delfino muso bianco; lagenorinco dal becco bianco.

 Weißschnauzen Delphin. Langfinnen Delphin; Langfinnendelphin; Weißschnauzendelphin; Weißschnauziger Delphin; Weißschnauziger Springer; Weißschnäuziger Delphin; Weißschnäuziger Springer.

 Dauphin à bec blanc. Béluga; dauphin à nez blanc; dauphin à rostre blanc; dauphin d'Eschricht; lagenorhynche à bec blanc; lagenorhynque à bec blanc.

 White-beaked dolphin. Eschricht's dolphin; jumper; scoulter; squidhound; white-beak; white-beaked bottlenose; white-beaked porpoise; white-nosed dolphin; whitebeak dolphin.

Lagenorhynchus is a compound of the Greek words *lagenos* (= bottle) and rhynchos (= nose; snout). Seen from above, the head and snout resemble the neck and flare of a bottle. *Albirostris* is a compound of the Latin words *albus* (= white) and *rostrum* (= nose; muzzle; snout); *bottlenose with a white snout.*

white beaked dolphin
Lagenorhynchus albirostris

ATLANTIC WHITE-SIDED DOLPHIN / *Lagenorhynchus acutus*

18

id
checklist

BODY: Powerfully built, black or dark-grey on top. Very thick tail stock. Grey stripe on sides. Yellow-green or bright yellow, oblong patch on tail stock. White spot in middle of side below dorsal fin. Rather short, abrupt snout, black on top and white underneath.

DORSAL FIN: Centrally situated, relatively high and sharp-pointed, especially on males, curves slightly aft.

FLIPPERS: Black or dark-grey, rather long and broad, but taper sharply.

FLUKES: notched in middle; pointed on ends.

DIVING: Usually takes shallow dives, breathing every 10 to 15 seconds.

BLOWING: Not discernible.

SWIMMING: Goes fast, sometimes with most of its body above surface when coming up to breathe.

HABITAT: Sometimes shallows although usually in deeper waters; preferred depth is 100 to 1,500 m.

NATURE: Often frolics. Sometimes follows ships and boats and even large whales.

Order:	Whales (Cetacea), 78 species.
Suborder:	Toothed whales (Odontoceti), 68 species.
Superfamily:	Dolphins (Delphinoidea), 40 species.
Family:	Delphinidae, 31 species.
Subfamily:	Delphininae, 14 species.
Genus:	Lagenorhynchus, 6 species.
Species:	L. acutus.

Length/weight (newborn):	1-1.3 m / 30-40 kg.
Length (adult):	♀ 1.9-2.43 m. ♂ 2.75 m.
Weight (adult):	♀ 150-182 kg. ♂ 165-235 kg.
Lifetime:	20-30 years, maybe 40.
World population:	Unknown.
In Icelandic waters:	38,000.
Group size:	(1) 10-100(1,000+).
Diet:	

Lagenorhynchus acutus (Gray, 1828).
Synonym: *Delphinus acutus, Delphinus eschrichtii, Delphinus leucopleurus, Electra acuta, Grampus acutus, Lagenorhynchus arcticus, Lagenorhynchus bombifrons, Lagenorhynchus gubernator, Lagenorhynchus leucopleurus, Lagenorhynchus perspicillatus, Leicopleurus arcticus, Leucopleurus arcticus.*

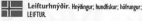
Leifturhnýðir. Hnýðingur; hundfiskur; höfrungur; LEIFTUR.

Kvitskjeving. Springer.

Delfín de flancos blancos del Atlantico. Delfín de lomo blanco.

Lagenorinco acuto. Delfino a fianchi bianchi; Lagenorinco dai fianchi bianchi.

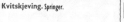
Weißseiten Delphin. Nordischer Delphin; Springer; Weißseitendelphin.

Dauphin à flancs blancs. Dauphin d'Eschricht; lagenorhynque à flancs de l'Atla.

Atlantic white-sided dolphin. Atlantic whiteside dolphin; Atlantic white-sided porpoise; Eschricht's dolphin; jumper; lag; springer; white-side; white-sided bottlenose; white-sided dolphin.

Lagenorhynchus is a compound of the Greek words *lagenos* (= bottle) and *rhynchos* (= nose; snout). Seen from above, the head and snout resemble the neck and flare of a bottle. *Acutus* is Latin (= sharp; narrow-pointed; acute); *bottlenose with a sharp-pointed dorsal fin.*

atlantic white sided dolphin
Lagenorhynchus acutus

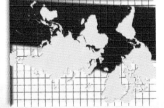

id checkLIST

BODY: Thin and completely streamlined. Mostly black or dark-grey on back. The colour forms a V-shaped pattern on the sides below the dorsal fin; yellowish forward on sides, light-grey on tail stock; looks like an hourglass lying on its side; white underneath. Snout rather long and narrow, clearly delineated from the relatively high forehead. The complex, clear pattern varies by ocean area.

DORSAL FIN: Sharply pointed and curving slightly aft, situated centrally, grey at base.

FLIPPERS: Black and tapered.

FLUKES: Grey or black on both sides.

DIVING: Usual duration is 10 seconds to 2 minutes; occasionally up to 8 minutes. Known to go as deep as 280 m in pursuit of food.

BLOWING: Not discernible.

SWIMMING: Swims fast and can reach high speed (up to 64 km per hour).

HABITAT: Occasionally enters shallow waters, but generally keeps to the deeps farther out; preferred depth unknown.

NATURE: Individual freedom generally more important with common dolphins than other species in this family; known for exuberance and aerobatics.

Order:	Whales (Cetacea), 78 species.
Suborder:	Toothed whales (Odontoceti), 68 species.
Superfamily:	Dolphins (Delphinoidea), 40 species.
Family:	Delphinidae, 31 species.
Subfamily:	Delphininae, 14 species.
Genus:	Delphinus, 1 species.
Species:	D. delphis.
Subspecies:	Possibly numerous.

Length/weight (newborn):	0.8-1.05 m / unknown.		
Length (adult):	♀ 1.7-2.3 m.	♂ 1.8-2.6 m.	
Weight (adult):	♀ 70-90 kg.	♂ 80-136 kg.	
Lifetime:	Unknown.		
World population:	Unknown.		
In Icelandic waters:	Unknown.		
Group size:	(1) 10-500(1,000+).		
Diet:			

Delphinus delphis (Linnaeus, 1758).
Synonym: *Delphinus albimanus, Delphinus algeriensis, Delphinus bairdii, Delphinus capensis, Delphinus delphis bairdii, Delphinus delphis balteatus, Delphinus delphis curvirostris, Delphinus delphis delphis, Delphinus delphis fusus, Delphinus delphis moschatus, Delphinus delphis ponticus, Delphinus delphis souverbianus, Delphinus delphis variegatus, Delphinus dussumieri, Delphinus forsteri, Delphinus frithii, Delphinus fulvifasciatus, Delphinus fulvofasciatus, Delphinus janira, Delphinus longirostris, Delphinus major, Delphinus marginatus, Delphinus microps, Delphinus moorei, Delphinus novaezealandiae, Delphinus novaezeelandiae, Delphinus novaezelandiae, Delphinus pomeegra, Delphinus roseiventris, Delphinus sao, Delphinus sowerbianus, Delphinus vulgaris, Delphinus walkeri, Delphinus zelandae, Eudelphinus tasmaniensis, Grampus sowerbianus.*

 Léttir. Barberi, EIGINLEGI HÖFRUNGUR; HUNDFISKUR; höfrungur; marsvin.

 Delfin. Springer; springkval.

 Delfín común. Arroaz común; arroaz; delfin; golfin; ruaso; tonina.

 Delfino comune. Delfino; tumberello.

 Gemeiner Delphin. Delphin; Gewöhnlicher Delphin; Meerschwein; Schnabelfisch.

 Dauphin commun. Bec d'oie; camus; dauphin; dauphin à bande fauve; dauphin bordé; dauphin des anciens; dauphin ordinaire; dauphin vulgaire; oie de mer.

Common dolphin. Atlantic dolphin; Cape dolphin; common ocean dolphin; criss-cross dolphin; crisscross dolphin; dolphin; dolphin of the Mediterranean; hourglass dolphin; Pacific dolphin; porpoise saddleback; saddleback dolphin; saddleback porpoise; white-bellied porpoise; whitebelly dolphin; whitebelly porpoise.

Delphinus is Latin (= dolphin; porpoise). *Delphis* is Greek (= porpoise), derived from *delphus* (= womb), suggesting the time when the Greeks worshipped dolphins as gods and, therefore, the source of life; *dolphin* (of Romans and Greeks) or *the true dolphin*.

common dolphin
Delphinus delphis

BOTTLENOSE DOLPHIN / Tursiops truncatus

22

id checklist

BODY: Very rakish build. Coloration varies by subspecies; commonly, however, mostly dark-grey on back, light-grey on sides and either pink or white underneath. Subspecies in the North Pacific often brown on top, rather than grey. Older animals often have patches on the underbelly. Snout is short and narrow, but clearly set off from the domed forehead. Lower jaw is longer than the upper one.

DORSAL FIN: Relatively high, centrally situated and crescent-shaped.

FLIPPERS: Rather small and tapered at end.

FLUKES: Arched, sharply pointed ends; notch in middle.

DIVING: Two ecological variations: shallow-water and open-ocean animals; former dives for 3 to 4 minutes at a time, while latter is believed capable of staying down longer and of diving to a depth of 600 m or even more hunting groundfish.

BLOWING: Not discernible.

SWIMMING: Powerful swimmer, capable of various swimming feats.

HABITAT: Either shallow water or deep.

NATURE: Can be very playful, jumping, for example, several metres into the air. Frequently follow ships and boats or keep company with sharks and large whales.

Order:	Whales (Cetacea), 78 species.
Suborder:	Toothed whales (Odontoceti), 68 species.
Superfamily:	Dolphins (Delphinoidea), 40 species.
Family:	Delphinidae, 31 species.
Subfamily:	Delphininae, 14 species.
Genus:	Tursiops, 1 species.
Species:	T. truncatus.
Subspecies:	At least T. t. truncatus, T. t. gilli and T. t. aduncus.

Length/weight (newborn):	0.84-1.3 m / 15-30 kg.
Length (adult):	♀ 1.9-3.67 m. ♂ 2.7-3.9 m.
Weight (adult):	♀ 150-350 kg. ♂ 275-650 kg.
Lifetime:	30 years.
World population:	Unknown.
In Icelandic waters:	Unknown.
Group size:	1, 2-25(1,000).
Diet:	

Tursiops truncatus (Montagu, 1821).
Synonym: *Beluga kingii, Delphinus abusalam, Delphinus aduncus, Delphinus caerulescens, Delphinus compressicauda, Delphinus cymodice, Delphinus cymodoce, Delphinus erebennus, Delphinus eurynome, Delphinus gadamu, Delphinus hamatus, Delphinus metis, Delphinus nesarnack, Delphinus nesarnak, Delphinus nesernack, Delphinus parvimanus, Delphinus perniger, Delphinus salam, Delphinus symodice, Delphinus troncatus, Delphinus truncatus, Delphinus tursio, Delphinus tursio obtusus, Sotalia gadamu, Sotalia perniger, Sousa gadamu, Steno gadamu, Steno perniger, Tursio catalania, Tursio cymodice, Tursio cymodoce, Tursio eurynome, Tursio metis, Tursio subridens, Tursio truncatus, Tursiops aduncus, Tursiops aduncus abusalam, Tursiops catalania, Tursiops cymodice, Tursiops dawsoni, Tursiops fergusoni, Tursiops gephyreus, Tursiops gilli, Tursiops gillii, Tursiops maugeanus, Tursiops nesarnack, Tursiops nesarnack catalania, Tursiops nuuanu, Tursiops parvimanus, Tursiops truncatus ponticus, Tursiops tursio.*

Tursiops is a compound of the Latin word *tursio* (= animal similar to a dolphin (from the writings of Plinius, the Elder); porpoise) and the Greek word *ops* or *opos* (= face). *Truncatus* is from the Latin word *trunco* or *truncare* (= cut off; shorten; truncate); *animal having a face like one cut off a porpoise.*

bottlenose dolphin
Tursiops truncatus

 Stökkull. Dettir; höfrungur; sprettfiskur.

 Tumler. Springer.

Delfin mular. Pez mular; mulá; tursión; tursio truncado; tursión.

Tursiope. Delfino maggiore; delfino soffiatore; tursione; tursiope troncato.

 Großer Tümmler. Flaschennase; Großer Delphin; Großtümmler; Nesarnak.

 Tursion soufleur. Dauphin à gros nez; dauphin nesarnak; dauphin souffleur; grand dauphin; grand souffleur; nésarnak; oudre; souffleur; souffleur vulgaire; tursion; tursiops tronqué.

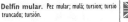 **Bottlenose dolphin.** Atlantic bottlenose dolphin; Atlantic bottle-nosed dolphin; black dolphin; black porpoise; bottlenose; bottlenose dolfin; bottlenose porpoise; bottle-nosed dolphin; bottlenosed dolphin; common bottlenose dolphin; common porpoise; cowfish; grey dolphin; grey porpoise; Pacific bottlenose dolphin; porpoise; southern bottle-nosed dolphin.

id checklist

BODY: Very slender and supple build, rather similar to common dolphin's (Delphinus delphis). Complex coloration. Generally dark-grey or brown on top or even bluish, sides light-grey or light-blue and underbelly pink or white. A dark stripe separates these areas, starting from the eyes and broadening close to the tail stock. Snout rather long and narrow, darkish. Tail stock rather narrow and unusually lightweight in appearance for a dolphin.

DORSAL FIN: Dark and rather tall and crescent-shaped.

FLIPPERS: Small, darkish and tapered.

FLUKES: Relatively small.

DIVING: Usually submerges for 5 to 10 minutes at a time, descending to at least a depth of 200 m.

BLOWING: Not discernible.

SWIMMING: Often hurtles along, sometimes jumping or doing other aerobatics.

HABITAT: Both shallow and deep waters; preferred depth unknown.

NATURE: Sportive and curious. Can jump to a height of 7 m and perform various aerobatics. Frequently follows ships and boats.

25

Order:	Whales (Cetacea), 78 species.
Suborder:	Toothed whales (Odontoceti), 68 species.
Superfamily:	Dolphins (Delphinoidea), 40 species.
Family:	Delphinidae, 31 species.
Subfamily:	Delphininae, 14 species.
Genus:	Stenella, 5 species.
Species:	S. coeruleoalba.

Length/weight (newborn):	1 m / unknown.
Length (adult):	♀ 1.8-2.2 m. ♂ 2-2.5 m.
Weight (adult):	♀ 90-120 kg. ♂ 120-156 kg.
Lifetime:	60 years.
World population:	Unknown.
In Icelandic waters:	Unknown.
Group size:	1 (5)-300(3,000).
Diet:	

Stenella coeruleoalba (Meyen 1833).
Synonym: *Clymene dorides, Clymene euphrosyne, Clymene similis, Clymenia aesthenops, Clymenia esthenops, Clymenia burmeisteri, Clymenia dorides, Clymenia euphrosyne, Clymenia euphrosynoides, Clymenia similis, Clymenia styx, Delphinus aesthenops, Delphinus albirostratus, Delphinus amphitriteus, Delphinus caeruloalbus, Delphinus caeruloalbus, Delphinus euphrosyne, Delphinus holboellii, Delphinus holbollii, Delphinus lateralis, Delphinus marginatus, Delphinus styx, Delphinus thyos, Lagenorhynchus caeruleoalbus, Lagenorhynchus lateralis, Lageno rhynchus caeruleoalbus, Orca tethyos, Prodelphinus amphitriteus, Prodelphinus burmeisteri, Prodelphinus caeruleoalbus, Prodelphinus caeruleoalbus euphrosyne, Prodelphinus doreides, Prodelphinus euphrosyne, Prodelphinus euphrosinoides, Prodelphinus euphrosyne, Prodelphinus lateralis, Prodelphinus marginatus, Prodelphinus petersii, Prodelphinus tethyos, Stenella caeruleoalbus, Stenella caeruleoalbus caeruleoalbus, Stenella euphrosyne.*

 Rákaskoppari. RÁKAHÖFRUNGUR; sprettingur.

 Stripedelfin. Springer; stripet delfin.

 Delfín listado. Delfin a rayas; delfin azul; delfin de betas; delfin rayado; estenela.

 Stenella striata. Delfino bianco-ceruleo; delfino dalle briglie; delfino eufrosine; prodelfino bianco-ceruleo.

 Blauweißer Delphin. Blau-Weißer Delphin; Streifendelphin.

 Dauphin bleu et blanc. Dauphin de Téthys; dauphin euphrosine; dauphin ragé.

 Striped dolphin. Black-jawed dolphin; blue dolphin; blue-white; blue-white dolphin; euphrosyne dolphin; Gray's dolphin; Gray's long-snouted porpoise; Greek dolphin; harnessed dolphin; longsnout; long-snouted dolphin; Meyen's dolphin; streaker; streaker porpoise; striped porpoise; styx dolphin; white-belly; white-belly porpoise.

Stenella is derived from the Greek word *stenos* (= tight; thin), thought to refer to the fact that the upper and lower jaws only just meet at the front of the snout. *Coeruleoalba* is a compound of the Latin words *caeruleus* (= dark-blue; sky-blue) and *albus* (= white); **the blue-white whale with jaws that barely touch or the blue-white narrow-nose.**

striped dolphin
Stenella coeruleoalba

id checklist

BODY: Considerable size difference between genders. Peculiarly pied body with clear colour divisions; mostly dark on top with, however, a greyish patch aft of the dorsal fin and on sides. A white disk behind each eye. Believed to be some differences in appearance between Northern and Southern Hemisphere stocks, especially regarding the dark coloration on top. In the Northern Hemisphere, the colour is coal-black, while in the Southern Hemisphere, it is dark-grey.

DORSAL FIN: Very high and straight, especially in old males (up to 2 m). Shorter and curved back on females.

FLIPPERS: Large and spatulate.

FLUKES: Broad, notched in middle. Black on top, white underneath. Can be ragged. Sharp-pointed ends.

DIVING: Generally lasts four or so minutes; migrating groups hunting seals and other marine mammals rather than fish. Can, however, dive for 5 to 15 minutes.

BLOWING: Low, spherical; visible in cold, calm weather.

SWIMMING: On average, swim at 10 to 15 km per hour; can, however, reach 55 km per hour, if necessary.

HABITAT: A shallow-water and open-ocean whale; wide distribution. Preferred depth 100 to 1,000 m.

NATURE: Often breaches and frolics on surface; well-known spyhopper.

MORE INFORMATION ON PAGE 68

Order:	Whales (Cetacea), 78 species.
Suborder:	Toothed whales (Odontoceti), 68 species.
Superfamily:	Dolphins (Delphinoidea), 40 species.
Family:	Delphinidae, 31 species.
Subfamily:	Globicephalinae, 7 species.
Genus:	Orcinus, 1 species.
Species:	O. orca.

Length/weight (newborn):	1.83-2.74 m / 180 kg.
Length (adult):	♀ 5.5-8.5 m. ♂ 7-9.8 m.
Weight (adult):	♀ 2.6-7.5 tons. ♂ 4.5-10 tons.
Lifetime:	100 years.
World population:	Unknown.
In Icelandic waters:	6,000 - 7,000.
Group size:	1,2-40(100+).
Diet:	

Orcinus orca (Linnaeus, 1758).
Synonym: Delphinus duhameli, Delphinus duhamelii, Delphinus gladiator, Delphinus grampus, Delphinus maximus, Delphinus (maximus) pinna in medio dorso, Delphinus minimus rostro, Delphinus orca, Delphinus orca ensidorsatus, Delphinus serra, Delphinus victorini, Grampus orca, Grampus rectipinna, Ophysia pacifica, Orca africana, Orca antarctica, Orca ater, Orca ater fusca, Orca atra, Orca capensis, Orca eschrichtii, Orca gladiator, Orca gladiator arcticus, Orca gladiator australis, Orca gladiator europaeus, Orca gladiator tasmaniensis, Orca latirostris, Orca magellanica, Orca minor, Orca orca magellanicus, Orca pacifica, Orca rectipinna, Orca rectispina, Orca schlegelii, Orca stenorhyncha, Orca tasmanica, Orcinus eschrichtii, Orcinus orca capensis, Orcinus orca eschrichti, Orcinus orca magellanicus, Orcinus schlegelii, Physeter microps.

 Háhyrningur. Barberi; flugfiskur; hafurhvalur; háhyrna, háskerðingur; hnýðingur (niðingur); hundfiskur (kálfarnir); vagnhvalur; vögnuhvalur; selfæla; selreki; skjaldblesi; skjaldhvalur; skjöldungur; sverðfiskur (gamlir tarfar); þollur.

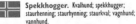 **Spekkhogger.** Kvalhund; spekkhugger; staurhenning; staurhynning; staurkval; vagnhund; vannhund.

Orca. Espadarte; espartón; espolarte; gladiator; grampo; latino; matador; orca común; orca espolarde; orca gladiator.

 Orca. Delfino gladiatore.

Schwertwal. Blutzkopf; Butzkopf; Gemeiner Schwertfisch; Großer Schwertwal; Großschwertwal; Mörder; Mörderdelphin; Orca; Schwert-Fisch; Schwertfisch.

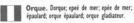 **Orque.** Dorque; epeé de mer; epée de mer; épaulard; orque épaulard; orque gladiator.

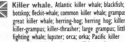 **Killer whale.** Atlantic killer whale; blackfish; botskop; fleckit-whale; common killer whale; grampus; great killer whale; herring-hog; herring hog; killer; killer-grampus; killer-thrasher; large grampus; little fighting whale; lupster; orca; orka; Pacific killer whale; pict-whale; sea-hog; swordfish; sword grampus; thornpelle; thornpoole; thrasher.

Orcinus is believed to be derived from either the Latin word orcus (= realm of the dead; hell) or the Latin word orchynus (= tunafish). Orca is thought to come from either the Latin word orcus (= realm of the dead; hell) or orca (= some whale). Others believe the Latin word orca is derived from the Greek words oryx, origos (=hook); the devil of the deep or the whale that follows tunafish or the whale resembling a tunafish (in its physical shape) or the whale that resembles a hook (because of the dorsal fin).

killer whale
Orcinus orca

LONG-FINNED PILOT WHALE / *Globicephala melas*

Distribution

id *checklist*

BODY: Mostly black; grey patch, however, aft of dorsal fin. White or light-grey stripe reaching along sides up to head, where the stripe splits, making an anchor-shaped pattern. Young animals' skin not as dark on top.

DORSAL FIN: High and rounded, especially on males.

FLIPPERS: Long and thin (18 to 27% of animal's total length), pointing aft.

FLUKES: Completely dark. Notched in middle; pointed ends.

DIVING: Seldom lasts more than 5 to 10 minutes, reaching depths of 30 to 60 m; can reach depths of 600 m.

BLOWING: Column about 1 m high; sound carries, and column visible in favourable weather.

SWIMMING: Usually swims slowly; animals often lie motionless on surface very close to each other.

HABITAT: Primarily a whale of the open ocean, apparently preferring a water temperature of 0° to 25°C; whale nevertheless enters shallows periodically, apparently in search of food. Preferred depth 300 to 1,500 m.

NATURE: Easily approached at sea, not wary of boats. Often lobtails. Frequently spyhops. Young animals sometimes breach.

Order:	Whales (Cetacea), 78 species.
Suborder:	Toothed whales (Odontoceti), 68 species.
Superfamily:	Dolphins (Delphinoidea), 40 species.
Family:	Delphinidae, 31 species.
Subfamily:	Globicephalinae, 7 species.
Genus:	Globicephala, 2 species.
Species:	G. melas.
Subspecies:	G. m. melas and G. m. edwardi.

Length/weight (newborn):	1.77-2 m / 70-80 kg.	
Length (adult):	♀ 4-6 m.	♂ 5.5-8.5 m.
Weight (adult):	♀ 1.8-3 tons.	♂ 3.5-5 tons.
Lifetime:	30-50 years, maybe 60.	
World population:	Unknown.	
In Icelandic waters:	100,000-200,000.	
Group size:	1, (2) 10-50(1,000+).	
Diet:		

Globicephala melas (Traill, 1809).
Synonym: *Delphinus carbonarius, Delphinus deductor, Delphinus fuscus, Delphinus globiceps, Delphinus grampus, Delphinus grinda, Delphinus harlani, Delphinus intermedius, Globicephala melas, Globicephala brachycephala, Globicephala indica, Globicephala leucosagmaphora, Globicephala macrorhyncha, Globicephala mela, Globicephala melaena, Globicephala melaena edwardi, Globicephala melaena melaena, Globicephala melas leucosagmaphora, Globicephala scammonii, Globicephala ventricosa, Globicephala affinis, Globicephalus australis, Globicephalus brachypterus, Globicephalus chilensis, Globicephalus conductor, Globicephalus edwardsii, Globicephalus fuscus, Globicephalus globiceps, Globicephalus guadoupensis, Globicephalus incrassatus, Globicephalus intermedius, Globicephalus macrorhynchus, Globicephalus melas, Globicephalus melas melas, Globicephalus propinquus, Globicephalus svineval, Globicephalus ventricosus, Globiceps affinis, Globiceps macrorhyncha, Globiceps melas, Grampus affinis, Phocaena edwardii, Phocaena edwardii.*

 Grindhvalur. Grind; MARSVÍN; strokkur.

 Grindkval.

 Calderón de aleta larga. Calderón común; calderón; calderón negro; cap d'olla; globicéfalo atlántica; vaca.

 Globicefalo. Globicefalo nero.

 Grindwal. Butskopf; Dummkopfwal; Grind; Pilotwal; Gewöhnlicher Grindwal; Pilotwal; Rundkopfwal; Schwarzer Delphin; Schwarzwal; Schwarzwal; Swinewal.

 Globicéphale Noir. Dauphin de Saint-Brieux; dauphin pilote; cachalot svineval; chaudron; conducteur; déducteur; épaulard à tête ronde; globicéphale; globicéphale conducteur; grinde; petit cachalot.

 Long-finned pilot whale. Atlantic blackfish; Atlantic pilot whale; bagfin; blackfish; black whale; bottlehead; bottle-nose; ca'ing whale; caa'ing whale; caaing whale; caa'ng whale; calling whale; common blackfish; common pilot whale; driving whale; drivingwhale; howling whale; Indian pilot whale; leading whale; longfin pilot whale; longfin; North Atlantic blackfish; Pacific blackfish; Pacific pilot whale; pilot whale; pothead; pothead whale; roundhead; social whale; thick-plated pilot whale.

Globicephala is a compound of the Latin word *globus* (= globe) and the Greek word *kephale* (= head). *Melas* is derived from the Greek word *melanus* (= black); **the bulbous headed black one.**

long-finned pilot whale
Globicephala melas

NORTHERN BOTTLENOSE WHALE / *Hyperoodon ampullatus*

Distribution

id checklist

BODY: Diverse colouring; generally grey-black or dark brown on upper body, but lighter on lower body. With age, some animals become very light-coloured all over, even white on the very high forehead and the small, but distinctive snout.

DORSAL FIN: About 30 cm high, situated far to the rear.

FLIPPERS: Just behind the head and very small.

FLUKES: Broad. No notch or slot in the middle.

DIVING: Generally dives for 14 to 70 minutes at a time. Longest time recorded for a dive is two hours. Generally, breathes for 10 minutes or so between dives.

BLOWING: Sends up a low, spherical column, 1 to 2 m high, at a slightly forward angle; distinct in clear weather.

SWIMMING: Generally swims slowly, but can move very fast if necessary.

HABITAT: Likes high seas best, keeping to the open ocean beyond continental shelf where depth is 1,000 to 2,000 m.

NATURE: Can be curious, approaching ships and boats.

Order:	Whales (*Cetacea*), 78 species.
Suborder:	Toothed whales (*Odontoceti*), 68 species.
Superfamily:	Beaked whales (*Ziphioidea*), 20 species.
Family:	*Ziphiidae*, 20 species.
Subfamily:	[None.]
Genus:	*Hyperoodon*, 2 species.
Species:	*H. ampullatus*.

Length/weight (newborn):	3-3.6 m / unknown.		
Length (adult):	♀ 7-8.7 m.	♂ 8.0-9.8 m.	
Weight (adult):	♀ 5.8-7 tons.	♂ 7.5-8.5 tons.	
Lifetime:	40-60 years.		
World population:	Unknown.		
In Icelandic waters:	42,000.		
Group size:	1, 2-10(35).		
Diet:			

Hyperoodon ampullatus (Forster, 1770).
Synonym: *Balaena ampullata, Balaena (minima) rostro longissimo et acutissimo, Balaena rostrata, Balaena rostro acutissimo, Cetodiodon hunteri, Chaenocetus rostratus, Chaerodelphinus edentulus, Delphinorhynchus rostratus, Delphinus bidens, Delphinus bidentatus, Delphinus butskode, Delphinus butskopf, Delphinus chemnitzianus, Delphinus diodon, Delphinus edentulus, Delphinus hunteri, Delphinus hyperoodon, Delphinus quadridens, Heterodon diodon, Hyperadon bidens, Hyperoodon baussardi, Hyperoodon bidens, Hyperoodon borealis, Hyperoodon butskop, Hyperoodon butzkoff, Hyperoodon butzkopf, Hyperoodon diodon, Hyperoodon honfloriensis, Hyperoodon latifrons, Hyperoodon rostratum, Hyperoodon rostratus, Lagenocetus latifrons, Lagocetus latifrons.*

Andarnefja. Andhvalur; döglingur; flugfiskur; mjaldur (gömul dýr); sandæta; svinhvalur.

Nebbkval. Andekval; bottlenos; stub.

Hocico de botella. Doglin.

Iperodonte boreale. Balena a becco, iperodonte del Nord.

Nördlicher Entenwal. Butskop; Butzkopf; Blutzkopf; Dogling; Dögling; Entenwal; Nördlicher Dögling; Schnabelfisch; Schwertfisch.

Hypéroodon boreal. Baleine à bec; baleine à bec commune; dauphin de honfleur; delphinorhynque à long bec; deugling; grand souffleur à bec d'oie; hyperodon; hyperodon arctique; hyperodon boréal; hypéroodon du Nord.

Northern bottlenose whale. Beaked whale; bottlehead; bottlenose whale; bottlenose; bottle-nosed whale; bottlenosed whale; common beaked whale; common bottle-nose; common bottlenose whale; flathead; flounder's head; North Atlantic bottlenose; North Atlantic bottlenosed whale; Northern bottle-nosed whale; steephead.

Hyperoodon is a compound of the Greek words *hyperoe* (= above) and *odon* (= tooth). *Ampullatus* is derived from the Latin word *ampulla* (= bottle). Seen from above, the head resembles the neck and flare of a bottle; the prominent-mouthed whale with the bottle-shaped head.

northern bottlenose whale
Hyperoodon ampullatus

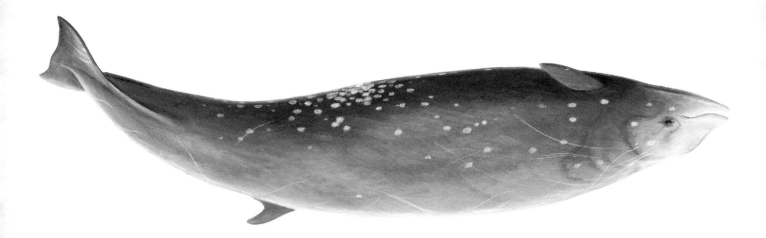

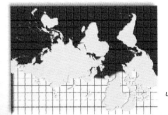

Distribution

CUVIER'S BEAKED WHALE / *Ziphius cavirostris*

32

id checklist

BODY: Diverse coloration, determined by gender, age or area. In the Pacific Ocean generally light-brown, while in the Atlantic light-grey or bluish. Smallish head is yellow-white, as is forward section of back. White patches on underbelly. Fully grown animals, especially males, covered with long, criss-crossed abrasions.

DORSAL FIN: Small. Either triangular or curved backward, situated rather far to rear.

FLIPPERS: Very small.

FLUKES: No notch in middle; lifted high for diving.

DIVING: Usually lasts about 40 minutes.

BLOWING: A low column, pointing a bit forward; visible especially after a long dive.

SWIMMING: On average, swims slowly, but capable of going fast, in which case its head usually shows. Dorsal fin usually visible.

HABITAT: A deep-sea whale, like its relatives; preferred depth, however, is not known.

NATURE: Known to breach, in which case the whole body emerges nearly vertically from the sea. Clumsy landing. Generally avoids boats and ships.

Order:	Whales (*Cetacea*), 78 species.
Suborder:	Toothed whales (*Odontoceti*), 68 species.
Superfamily:	Beaked whales (*Ziphioidea*), 20 species.
Family:	*Ziphiidae*, 20 species.
Subfamily:	[None.]
Genus:	*Ziphius*, 1 species.
Species:	*Z. cavirostris*.

Length/weight (newborn):	2-3 m / 250 kg.
Length (adult):	♀ 7.5 m. ♂ 5-6.93 m.
Weight (adult):	♀ 3-6 tons. ♂ 2-5 tons.
Lifetime:	60-70 years.
World population:	Unknown.
In Icelandic waters:	Unknown.
Group size:	1 (adult male), 3-10(25).
Diet:	

Ziphius cavirostris (G. Cuvier, 1823).
Synonym: *Aliama desmaresti, Aliama indica, Delphinus desmaresti, Delphinus philippii, Delphinorhynchus australis, Epiodon australe, Epiodon australis, Epiodon cathamiensis, Epiodon cryptodon, Epiodon desmarestii, Epiodon heraultii, Epiodon patachonicum, Hyperodon semijunctus, Hyperondon semijunctus, Hyperoodon capensis, Hyperoodon desmarestii, Hyperoodon doumetii, Hyperoodon gervaisi, Hyperoodon gervaisii, Hyperoodon semijunctus, Petrorhynchus capensis, Petrorhynchus indicus, Petrorhynchus mediterraneus, Ziphiorrhynchus cryptodon, Ziphius aresques, Ziphius australis, Ziphius cavirostris indicus, Ziphius chatamensis, Ziphius chathamensis, Ziphius cryptodon, Ziphius decavirostris, Ziphius grebnitzkii, Ziphius indicus, Ziphius novaezealandiae, Ziphius savii, Zyphius chathamensis.*

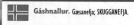

Gáshnallur. Gæsanefja; SKUGGANEFJA.

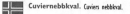

Cuviernebbkval. Cuviers nebbkval.

Zifio comun. Ballena de Cuvier; zifio; zifio común; zifio de Cuvier.

Zifio.

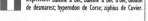

Cuviers-Schnabelwal. Cuviers Wal; Schnabelwal.

Ziphius. Baleine à bec; baleine à bec d'oie; diodon de desmarest; hyperodon de Corse; ziphius de Cuvier.

Cuvier's beaked whale. Cuvier's whale; goosebeak; goose-beaked whale; goose beaked whale; two-toothed beaked whale.

Ziphius is believed to have come from the Greek word *xiphias* (= swordfish) or *xiphos* (= sword). *Cavirostris* is a compound of the Latin words *cavus* (= hollow (inside)) and *rostrum* (= nose; muzzle; snout); *sword whale with hollow snout.*

cuvier's beaked whale
Ziphius cavirostris

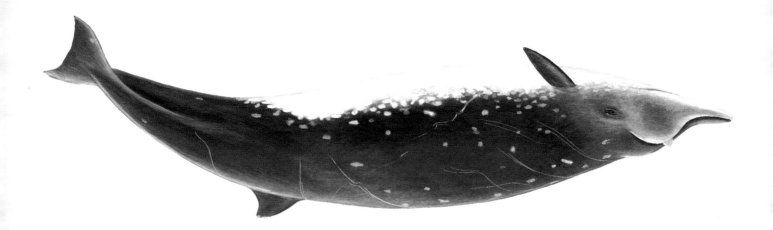

Distribution

BLAINVILLE'S BEAKED WHALE / *Mesoplodon densirostris*

id checklist

BODY: Fully grown animals are black or dark-grey on the back and sides, but light-coloured on the snout and underbelly; body, especially on males, is often covered with grey-white, pink and yellow oblong and circular patches and scratches. Relatively thick and rather long snout. Lower jaw is longer than the upper jaw, forming a high arch. Has two large, sharply pointed teeth sticking out from the back of the lower jaw.

DORSAL FIN: Very small, curving slightly aft and situated far to rear.

FLIPPERS: Rather insubstantial.

FLUKES: Approximately 1 m wide, no notch. Sharply pointed ends.

DIVING: Generally for 20 to 45 minutes; goes very deep. When animal resurfaces, the nose emerges first, nearly vertical.

BLOWING: Usually hardly discernible.

SWIMMING: Sometimes slaps its snout on the surface and turns over.

HABITAT: A deep-sea whale, like others in its family; preferred depth is unknown.

NATURE: Believed to be withdrawn and shy.

Order:	Whales (*Cetacea*), 78 species.
Suborder:	Toothed whales (*Odontoceti*), 68 species.
Superfamily:	Beaked whales (*Ziphioidea*), 20 species.
Family:	Ziphiidae, 20 species.
Subfamily:	[None.]
Genus:	Mesoplodon, 14 species.
Species:	M. densirostris.

Length/weight (newborn):	1.9-2.6 m / 60 kg.	
Length (adult):	♀ 4.7 m.	♂ 6 m.
Weight (adult):	♀ 1 ton.	♂ 3.5 tons.
Lifetime:	Unknown.	
World population:	Unknown.	
In Icelandic waters:	Unknown.	
Group size:	1, 2-10.	
Diet:	( )	

Mesoplodon densirostris (Blainville, 1817).
Synonym: *Delphinus densirostris, Nodus densirostris, Ziphius sechellensis.*

 Króksnjáldri. Grófsnjáldri.

 Blainvillespisskval. Blainvilles spisskval.

Zifio de Blainville.

Mesoplodonte di Blainville.

 Blainville-Zweizahnwal.

Mesoplodon de Blainville.

 Blainville's beaked whale. Atlantic beaked whale; Blainville's whale; cowfish; dense-beaked whale; tropical beaked whale.

Mesoplodon is the Greek words *mesos* (= middle), *hopla* (= arms, weapons) and *odon* (= tooth) or *mesos* (= middle), *ploe* (= floating) and *odon* (= tooth). Densirostris is a compound of the Latin words *densus* (= dense) og *rostrum* (= nose, muzzle, snout); *the whale armed with a tooth in the lower mid-jaw and very densely built.*

blainville's beaked whale
Mesoplodon densirostris

35

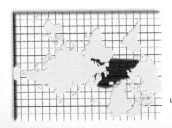

 Distribution

SOWERBY'S BEAKED WHALE / *Mesoplodon bidens*

id
checklist

BODY: Resembles a torpedo. Fully grown animals dark-grey or bluish on top, lighter undernearth; whitish spots cover body. Younger animals are lighter in colour and have fewer spots. Long and slender snout. Few scratches and abrasions mark the body. Dark around eyes. Teeth very visible in centre of lower jaw. Bulge in front of blowhole.

DORSAL FIN: Small, situated aft of middle; sometimes considerably bowed.

FLIPPERS: Proportionally long, compared with other species in family.

FLUKES: No notch.

DIVING: Goes very deep.

BLOWING: Low and spherical; visible in favourable conditions.

SWIMMING: Emerges from dives nearly vertical.

HABITAT: Keeps to open ocean like other species in the family; preferred depth unknown.

NATURE: Does not show itself much, believed to be shy.

Order:	Whales (*Cetacea*), 78 species.
Suborder:	Toothed whales (*Odontoceti*), 68 species.
Superfamily:	Beaked whales (*Ziphioidea*), 20 species.
Family:	*Ziphiidae*, 20 species.
Subfamily:	[None.]
Genus:	*Mesoplodon*, 14 species.
Species:	M. bidens.

Length/weight (newborn):	2.4-2.7 m / 170-200 kg.	
Length (adult):	♀ 5.1 m.	♂ 5.5 m.
Weight (adult):	♀ 1 ton.	♂ 1.3-1.5 tons.
Lifetime:	Unknown.	
World population:	Unknown.	
In Icelandic waters:	Unknown.	
Group size:	1, 2-10.	
Diet:		

Mesoplodon bidens (Sowerby, 1804).
Synonym: *Aodon dalei, Delphinorhynchus micropterus, Delphinorhynchus sowerbyi, Delphinus micropteron, Delphinus micropterus, Delphinus sowerbensis, Delphinus sowerbi, Delphinus sowerbyensis, Delphinus sowerbyi, Diodon sowerbaei, Diodon sowerbi, Diodon sowerbyi, Heterodon dalei, Mesiodiodon sowerbyi, Mesoplodon sowerbensis, Mesoplodon sowerbiensis, Micropteron bidens, Micropteron sowerbiensis, Nodus dalei, Physeter bidens, Ziphius sowerbiensis.*

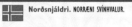
Norðsnjáldri. NORRÆNI SVÍNHVALUR.

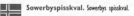
Sowerbyspisskval. Sowerbys spisskval.

Zifio de Sowerby.

Mesoplodonte di Sowerby. Mesoplodonte bidente.

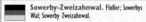
Sowerby-Zweizahnwal. Floßer; Sowerbys Wal; Sowerby Zweizahnwal.

Mesoplodon de Sowerby. Baleine à bec de Sowerby; dauphin de Dale; dauphin de Havre; dauphin de Hâvre.

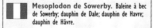
Sowerby's beaked whale. Sowerby's whale; North Sea beaked whale; cowfish.

Mesoplodon is either of the Greek words *mesos* (= middle), *hopla* (= arms, weapons) and *odon* (= tooth) or *mesos* (= middle), *ploe* (= floating) and *odon* (= tooth). *Bidens* is a compound of the Latin words *bi* (= twice) and *dens* (= tooth); *the whale armed with a tooth in the mid-lower jaw and acually two* or *the whale with a tooth "floating" in the lower jaw, actually two.*

sowerby's beaked whale
Mesoplodon bidens

MORE INFORMATION ON PAGE 78

id *checklist*

BODY: Dark-brown or dark-grey on top, lighter on sides; fully grown animals often have scars or abrasions from giant squid, especially on head.
DORSAL FIN: Very insubstantial, situated aft of centre; knobs between dorsal fin and flukes.
FLIPPERS: Relatively small.
FLUKES: Enormous and broad; lifted high before whale dives.
DIVING: Dives vertically, often remaining submerged for long periods (up to two hours, although usually under 45 minutes). Commonly reappears in nearly the same place it started from; usually waits from 5 to 15 minutes and up to one hour before diving again.
BLOWING: Seen from the side, the blow points forward, seen from the front, it angles to the right. The blowhole, on the left, is very far forward on the head.
SWIMMING: Often lies motionless on the surface; otherwise, swims about slowly; can reach great speed if necessary.
HABITAT: Primarily a deep-sea whale; preferred depth 300 to 1,500 m.
NATURE: Frequently breaches high in the air, especially young animals during bad weather.

Order:	Whales (Cetacea), 78 species.
Suborder:	Toothed whales (Odontoceti), 68 species.
Superfamily:	Physeteroidea, 3 species.
Family:	Physeteridae, 3 species.
Subfamily:	[None.]
Genus:	Physeter, 1 species.
Species:	P. macrocephalus.

A sperm whale from the treatise of Jón the Learned, On Iceland's Diverse Nature, 1640.

Length/weight (newborn):	3.5-4.5 m / 1 ton.
Length (adult):	♀ 8-17 m. ♂ 17-20 m.
Weight (adult):	♀ 20-38 tons. ♂ 40-52 tons.
Lifetime:	60-80 years.
World population:	1,500,000-2,000,000.
In Icelandic waters:	1,400.
Group size:	1, 2-50+.
Diet:	

Physeter macrocephalus (Linnaeus, 1758).
Synonym: Catodon australis, Catodon colneti, Catodon krefftii, Catodon macrocephalus, Catodon polycyctus, Catodon polycyphus, Catodon polyscyphus, Catodon svineval, Cetus cylindricus, Delphinus bayeri, Meganeuron kreftii, Phiseter cylindricus, Phiseter mular, Phiseter trumpo, Physalus cylindricus, Physeter andersonii, Physeter australasianus, Physeter australis asiaticus, Physeter australis, Physeter catodon, Physeter catodon australis, Physeter catodon catodon, Physeter gibbosus, Physeter krefftii, Physeter macrocephalus cinereus, Physeter macrocephalus niger, Physeter maximus, Physeter microps, Physeter microps falcidentatus, Physeter microps rectidentatus, Physeter novae angliae, Physeter orthodon, Physeter polycephus, Physeter polycystus, Physeter pterodon, Physeter tursio, Physererus sulcatus, Tursio vulgaris.

 Búrhvalur. BÚRHVELI; BÚRI; durnir; fjósi; hólmafiskur; morðhvalur; nauthvalur; nauthveli; nautshvalur; skarði; svinhvalur.

 Spermkval. Kaskelott; potkval; sperm; spermasettkval.

 Cachalote. Cachalot; cachalote macrocéfalo; cap-gros; pex mular.

 Capodoglio. Capidoglio; capidolio.

 Pottwal. Cachalot; Großer Pottwal; Großköpfiger Walfisch; Kaschelot; Pottfisch.

 Cachalot. Cachalot à dents en faucille; cachalot à dents pointues; cachalot de la Nouvelle Angleterre; cachalot grosse tête; cachalot macrocéphale; grand cachalot; physeter.

 Sperm whale. Black fish; blunt-head cachalot; cachalot; cachelot; cachelot whale; great sperm whale; high-finned cachalot; pot whale; pottwhale; sea-guap; spermacet whale; spermaceti whale.

Physeter comes from the Greek word *physeter* (= blower), which is derived from *phuseter* (= eddy; whirlpool). *Macrocephalus* is a compound of the Greek words *makros* (= long; big) and *kephale* (= head); **the blower with the long head** or **the big-headed blower.**

sperm whale
Physeter macrocephalus

BOWHEAD WHALE / *Balaena mysticetus*

id
checklist

BODY: Mostly black or dark-brown; front of lower jaw, however, is white, often with irregular dark patches. Sometimes there is a grey belt around the narrowest part of the tail stock. Head is enormous, more than one-third of animal's total length. No callosities on head or elsewhere. Line of mouth arched. Indentation in head just behind blowhole.

DORSAL FIN: None.

FLIPPERS: Rounded and broad.

FLUKES: Prodigiously large, notched in middle; pointed ends.

DIVING: Usually cruises just below surface, diving for 4 to 20 minutes at a time. Can stay under longer and dive to depths of over 200 m. Often resurfaces where dive began.

BLOWING: V-shaped column; can reach a height of 6 m.

SWIMMING: Very slow swimmer, travelling at only 2 to 7 km per hour on long journeys.

HABITAT: Hunts in both shallow and deep waters in the polar seas of the North, though generally staying close to land.

NATURE: Sometimes breach, slap their flippers, lobtail and spyhop sometimes.

Order:	Whales (Cetacea), 78 species.
Suborder:	Baleen whales (Mysticeti), 10 species.
Superfamily:	[None.]
Family:	Balaenidae, 2 species.
Subfamily:	[None.]
Genus:	Balaena, 1 species.
Species:	B. mysticetus.

Length/weight (newborn):	3.5-4.5 m / unknown.
Length (adult):	♀ 14.5-20 m. ♂ 14-18 m.
Weight (adult):	♀ 70-120 tons. ♂ 60-90 tons.
Lifetime:	30-70 years.
World population:	3,000-12,000.
In Icelandic waters:	An occasional guest.
Group size:	1, 2-10(50).
Diet:	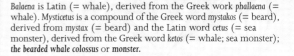

Balaena mysticetus (Linnaeus, 1758).
Synonym: *Balaena borealis, Balaena groenlandica, Balaena mysticetus arctica, Balaena mysticetus borealis, Balaena mysticetus groenlandica, Balaena mysticetus pitlekajensis, Balaena mysticetus pittekajensis, Balaena mysticetus roysii, Balaena vulgaris.*

 Norðhvalur. Grænlandshvalur; GRÆNLANDSSLÉTTBAKUR; sléttbakur; vatnshvalur.

  Grønlandskval. Huskval; nordkval; tuekval.

Ballena de Groenlandia. Cabeza arquaeda.

 Balena della Groenlandia. Balena boreale.

 Grönlandwal. Bartenwal; Bogenkopf; Grönländischer Walfisch; Grönlandswal; Nordwal; Polarwal; Wal; Walfisch.

 Baleine du Groenland. Baleine; baleine boréale; baleine de grande baie; baleine du Nord; baleine franche; baleine franche boréale; baleine franche du Groenland; baleine vraie.

 Bowhead whale. Arctic right whale; Arctic whale; bowhead; common whale; great polar whale; Greenland right whale; Greenland whale; ice whale; right whale; whalebone whale.

Balaena is Latin (= whale), derived from the Greek work *phallaena* (= whale). *Mysticetus* is a compound of the Greek word *mystakos* (= beard), derived from *mystax* (= beard) and the Latin word *cetus* (= sea monster), derived from the Greek word *ketos* (= whale; sea monster); **the bearded whale colossus** or **monster.**

bowhead whale
Balaena mysticetus

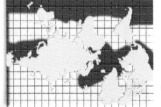

Distribution

id checklist

BODY: Rounded and spindle-shaped, tending toward stout; predominant colour is black, although can sometimes approach brown tones. Circumference where the whale is largest is about 60% of its length. Head is large, accounting for about one-third of the animal's total length. From the snout to its blowholes above eyes and on sides of lower jaw, there is a row of coarse growths, often called callosities. Some hair grows on snout, both on the upper and lower jaws. Mouth is enormous and built so that the animal can never close it completely; line of mouth very arched. In certain seasons, the skin on the backs of some animals flakes, so that they become white-speckled.

DORSAL FIN: None.

FLIPPERS: Quite long, wide and rounded.

FLUKES: Huge, with a prominent notch in the middle. Raised above surface before whale dives.

DIVING: Can dive for one hour.

BLOWING: Two columns, forming "V", reaching up to a height of 5 m.

SWIMMING: Usually swims slowly, paddling at 4 to 7 km per hour.

HABITAT: Preferred depth is 100 to 1,000 m.

NATURE: Easy to approach. Breaches often; splash audible from a distance of up to 1 km.

Order:	Whales (Cetacea), 78 species.
Suborder:	Baleen whales (Mysticeti), 10 species.
Superfamily:	[None.]
Family:	Balaenidae, 2 species.
Genus:	Eubalaena, 1 species.
Species:	E. glacialis.
Subspecies:	E. g. glacialis, E. g. australis and E. g. japonica.

Right whale from Jón Gudmundsson the Learned, 1640.

Length/weight (newborn):	4.5-6 m / 1 ton.
Length (adult):	♀ 18-18.5 m. ♂ 11-16.4 m.
Weight (adult):	♀ 60-80 tons. ♂ 30-60 tons.
Lifetime:	30-70 years.
World population:	4,000-5,500.
In Icelandic waters:	Rare.
Group size:	1, 2-12(100).
Diet:	

Eubalaena glacialis (Müller, 1776).
Synonym: *Balaena aleoutiensis, Balaena alutiensis, Balaena antarctica, Balaena antipodarum, Balaena antipodum, Balaena australis, Balaena biscayensis, Balaena britannica, Balaena capensis, Balaena cisarctica, Balaena culammak, Balaena cullamach, Balaena cullamacha, Balaena dorso impenni, Balaena eubalaena, Balaena euskariensis, Balaena glacialis, Balaena glacialis australis, Balaena hectori, Balaena islandica, Balaena japonica, Balaena kuliomoch, Balaena lunulata, Balaena grönlandica, Balaena mediterranea, Balaena mysticetus angulata, Balaena mysticetus antarctica, Balaena mysticetus islandica, Balaena nordcaper, Balaena sieboldii, Balaena tarentina, Balaena van benedeniana, Balaena van benedonia, Balaena vulgaris, Balaenoptera antarctica, Caperea antipodarum, Eubalaena australis, Eubalaena capensis, Eubalaena glacialis sieboldii, Eubalaena sieboldii, Hunterius svedenborgii, Hunterius temminckii, Hunterus temminckii, Macleayius australiensis, Macleayius britannicus.*

Sléttbakur. Hafurfiskur; hafurhvalur; hafurkitti; hafurkytti; hoddunefur; hraunhvalur; höddunefur; ÍSLANDSSLÉTTBAKUR; norðkaprari; vaðfiskur; vatnshvalur.

Nordkaper. Biscayerkval; rettkval; slettbak; slettbakkval.

Ballena franca. Balena; ballena; ballena atlántica; ballena de vizcaya; ballena vasca.

Balena franca boreale. Balena artica; balena del baschi; balena franca; balena nera.

Nordkaper. Biskayawal; Biskayerwal; Japanwal, Nordcaper; Nordatlantischer Glattwal; Südlicher Glattwal.

Baleine de Biscaye. Baleine de Basques; baleine des Basques; baleine d'Islande; baleine du Biscaye; baleine du Cap; baleine franche; baleine franche noir; baleine Japonaise; baleine sarde; sarde.

Right whale. Atlantic right whale; Biskay right whale; Biscay whale; Biscayan right whale; Biscayan whale; black right whale; black whale; great right whale; nordcaper; North-Atlantic right whale; North Atlantic right whale; north cape whale; North-Pacific right whale; North Pacific right whale; northern right whale; Pacific right whale; rock-nosed whale; sarde.

Eubalaena is a compound of the Latin words *eu* (= proper; true) and *balaena* (= whale), which is derived from the Greek word *phallaena* (= whale). *Glacialis* is derived from the Latin world *glacies* (= ice); the one and only true ice whale or the right whale associated with ice (that is, living in the coldest waters).

right whale
Eubalaena glacialis

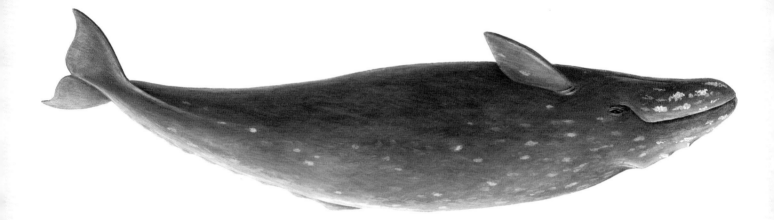

GRAY WHALE / *Eschrichtius robustus*

44

id *checklist*

BODY: Long and relatively thin, but strong and rough, mostly grey and covered with yellow or white flecks. Row of nodules on back of tail stock, not unlike the humpback and sperm whales. Head tapered and arched. Callosities on snout and sides.

DORSAL FIN: None, only a small hump.

FLIPPERS: Short and broad, but tapering toward ends.

FLUKES: Broad, deeply notched; somewhat pointed ends. Animal lifts flukes into air before diving, except in shallows.

DIVING: On long journeys, lasts 3 to 5 minutes, but for up to 18 minutes when searching for food.

BLOWING: V- or heart-shaped column (seen from rear or front of the animal), reaching up 3 to 4.5 m.

SWIMMING: On long journeys swims at an average 8 km per hour.

HABITAT: A whale of shallow waters; preferred depth 5 to 100 m.

NATURE: Very playful. Lobtails, spyhops frequently and often breaches. Curious and easy to approach.

Order:	Whales (*Cetacea*), 78 species.
Suborder:	Baleen whales (*Mysticeti*), 10 species.
Superfamily:	[None.]
Family:	Eschrichtiidae, 1 species.
Subfamily:	[None.]
Genus:	*Eschrichtius*, 1 species.
Species:	*E. robustus*.

Gray whale from Jón Gudmundsson the Learned, 1640.

Length/weight (newborn):	4.5-5 m / 500 kg.
Length (adult):	♀ 11-15 m. ♂ 11-14.6 m.
Weight (adult):	♀ 30-35 tons. ♂ 16 tons.
Lifetime:	80 years.
World population:	15,000-25,000.
In Icelandic waters:	Extinct.
Group size:	1, 2-18(50).
Diet:	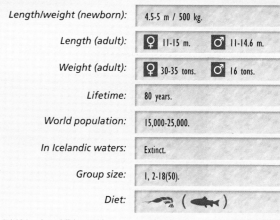

Eschrichtius robustus (Lilljeborg, 1861).
Synonym: *Agaphelus glaucus, Balaena boops, Balaena gibbosa, Balaenoptera physalus, Balaenoptera robusta, Eschrichtius gibbosus, Eschrichtius glaucus, Rhachianectes glaucus*.

 Sandlægja. GRÁHVALUR; sandæta.

 Gråkval. Kalifornisk gråkval.

 Ballena gris.

 Balena grigia. Balenottera grigia.

 Grauwal. Knotenfisch.

 Baleine grise. Baleine à six bosses; baleine de Californie; baleine gris de Californie.

 Gray whale. California gray whale; Californian gray whale; Californian grey whale; devil fish; devilfish; gray back; grey whale; hard head; mossback; musseldigger; mussel digger; Pacific gray whale; rip sack; rip sacks; scrag whale.

Eschrichtius comes from the name of the 19th century zoologist, Daniel Frederick Eschricht, a professor in Copenhagen. *Robustus* is Latin (= robust, strong); the robust or strongly built whale, named after Eschricht.

gray whale
Eschrichtius robustus

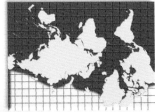

HUMPBACK WHALE / *Megaptera novaeangliae*

id checkLIST

BODY: No two exactly the same. Most common colour is black or dark-grey on the back and sides. Callosities (growths) on snout and top of head and on the forward edge of flippers.

DORSAL FIN: Rather small, situated just aft of the middle; can be variously shaped, e.g., broad and triangular or narrow and crescent-shaped or anything in-between.

FLIPPERS: Enormous, black or white or a combination of the two colours. Jagged along forward edges.

FLUKES: Very large, split in middle and often very jagged; extremely diverse coloration on underside, sometimes completely dark, but most often somewhat light-coloured or white. Tail stock is covered with barnacles up to the dorsal fin, not unlike the sperm and Gray whales.

DIVING: Usually submerged for 3 to 9 minutes at a time; can, however, stay down for up to 45 minutes.

BLOWING: Column (2.5 to 3 m) often very distinct, spherical.

SWIMMING: Usually swims slowly, but can go fast if necessary.

HABITAT: Both shallow waters and the open ocean; preferred depth 200 to 600 m.

NATURE: Often breaches and frolics on surface. Can be curious.

Order:	Whales (Cetacea), 78 species.
Suborder:	Baleen whales (Mysticeti), 10 species.
Superfamily:	[None.]
Family:	Rorquals (Balaenopteridae), 6 species.
Subfamily:	Megapterinae, 1 species.
Genus:	Megaptera, 1 species.
Species:	M. novaeangliae.

A "síldreki" in the treatise of Jón the Learned, On Iceland's Diverse Nature, 1640. This is obviously a humpback whale.

Length/weight (newborn):	4-5 m / 500 kg.
Length (adult):	♀ 14-19 m. ♂ 11.5-17.5 m.
Weight (adult):	♀ 30-48 tons. ♂ 25-35 tons.
Lifetime:	95 years.
World population:	10,000-250,000.
In Icelandic waters:	1,800.
Group size:	1, 2-3(20).
Diet:	

Megaptera novaeangliae (Borowski, 1781).
Synonym: *Balaena allamack, Balaena atlanticus, Balaena boops, Balaena gibbosa, Balaena lalandii, Balaena longimana, Balaena nodosa, Balaena novaeangliae, Balaena sulcata antarctica, Balaenoptera antarctica, Balaenoptera astrolabae, Balaenoptera australis, Balaenoptera capensis, Balaenoptera leucopteron, Balaenoptera syncondylus, Kyphobalaena keporkak, Megaptera americana, Megaptera antarctica, Megaptera australis, Megaptera bellicosa, Megaptera boops, Megaptera brasiliensis, Megaptera braziliensis, Megaptera burmeisteri, Megaptera gigas, Megaptera indica, Megaptera kusira, Megaptera kuzira, Megaptera lalandii, Megaptera longimana, Megaptera longimana moorei, Megaptera longipinna, Megaptera nodosa, Megaptera nodosa bellicosa, Megaptera nodosa lalandii, Megaptera nodosa nodosa, Megaptera nodosa novaezealandiae, Megaptera novaezelandiae, Megaptera osphyia, Megaptera poeskop, Megaptera versabilis, Poescopia lalandii, Rorqualus antarcticus, Rorqualus australis.*

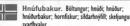 **Hnúfubakur.** Böltungur; hnúði; hnúður; hnúðurbakur; hornfiskur; síldarhnýfill; skeljungur; svarlhvalur.

Knølkval. Knøl; troldkval.

Ballena jarobada. Ballena; ballena nudosa; ballenato; jarobada; jubarta; megáptero de nueva inglaterra; xibarte; yubarta.

Megattera. Balenottera gobba.

Buckelwal. Jubarte; Knurrwal; Langflossenwal; Langflossiger; Finnfisch; Pflochfisch.

Mégaptère. Baleine à bosse; baleine à taquet; baleine tampon; gibbar; jubarte; rorqual à bosse.

Humpback whale. Aliama; anarnak; bunch; bunch whale; hump; hump back; humpback; hump-backed whale; humpbacked whale; hump whale; hunchbacked whale; Johnston's humpbached whale; keporkak; trouble.

Megaptera is a compound of the Greek words *megas* (= big) and *pteron* (= wing, in this instance, flippers). *Novaeangliae* is a compound of the Latin words *novus* (= new) and *anglia* (= England). **The big-flipper from New England** (that is, the north-east part of the United States: Maine, New Hampshire, Vermont, Massachusetts, Rhode Island and Connecticut).

humpback whale
Megaptera novaeangliae

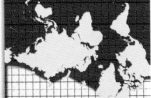

BLUE WHALE / *Balaenoptera musculus*

48

id *checklist*

BODY: Enormous. Slender and supple build, oblong and thin; mostly dark-grey or blue-grey all over with some light mottling on the sides. Head is relatively small and flat with ridge in front of blowhole. Tail stock unusually thick.

DORSAL FIN: Very small, only 30 cm high, situated toward rear; shape varies.

FLIPPERS: Long and narrow, white underneath and sometimes also on the front edges.

FLUKES: Large and broad, sometimes lifted above surface before whale dives.

DIVING: Duration, on average, 10 to 15 minutes, depth of 50 to 100 m.

BLOWING: High, straight column, rising 6 to 12 m.

SWIMMING: 2 to 6.5 km per hour while hunting food and 5 to 14 km per hour on long journeys. When fleeing, can reach speeds of up to 30 km per hour.

HABITAT: Keeps to open ocean; preferred depth is 200 to 800 m.

NATURE: Rather timid nature. No aerobatics.

Order:	Whales (Cetacea), 78 species.
Suborder:	Baleen whales (Mysticeti), 10 species.
Family:	Rorquals (Balaenopteridae), 6 species.
Subfamily:	Balaenopterinae, 5 species.
Order:	Balaenoptera, 5 species.
Species:	B. musculus.
Subspecies:	B. m. brevicauda, B. m. musculus and B. m. intermedia.

A blue whale from the treatise of Jón the Learned, On Iceland's Diverse Nature, 1640.

Length/weight (newborn):	6-7 m / 2.5 tons.
Length (adult):	♀ 22-33.58 m. ♂ 21-31 m.
Weight (adult):	♀ 110-190 tons. ♂ 100-160 tons.
Lifetime:	100 years.
World population:	6,000-14,000.
In Icelandic waters:	1,000.
Group size:	1, 2(5).
Diet:	

Balaenoptera musculus (Linnaeus, 1758).
Synonym: *Balaena borealis, Balaena (maxima) ventre plicato, Balaena maximus borealis, Balaena musculus, Balaena musculus (maxima), Balaenoptera arctica, Balaenoptera carolinae, Balaenoptera gigas, Balaenoptera indica, Balaenoptera intermedia, Balaenoptera jubartes, Balaenoptera miramaris, Balaenoptera rorqual, Balaenoptera sibaldii, Balaenoptera sibbaldi, Nalaenoptera jubartes, Physalus latirostris, Physalus sibbaldi, Physalus sibbaldii, Pterobalaena gigas, Pterobalaena gryphus, Rorqualus boops, Rorqualus borealis, Rorqualus major, Rorqualus sibbaldii, Sibbaldius antarcticus, Sibbaldius sulfureus, Sibbaldius borealis, Sibbaldus musculus.*

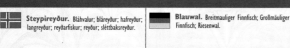

Steypireyður. Bláhvalur; bláreyður; hafreyður; langreyður; reyðarfiskur; reyður; sléttbaksreyður.

Blákval.

Ballena azul. Rorcual gigante.

Blauwal. Breitmauliger Finnfisch; Großmäuliger Finnfisch; Riesenwal.

Rorqual bleu. Baleine bleue; baleine d'Ostende; baleine jubarte; baleinoptère bleu; baleinoptère jubarte; grand rorqual; grande baleine bleue; jubarte, rorqual à ventre cannelé; rorqual de Sibbald.

Blue whale. Blue rorqual; broad-nosed whale; great blue whale; great northern rorqual; ostende whale; Sibbald's rorqual; sulphur-bottom; sulphurbottom; sulfur-bottom whale; sulphurbottom whale.

Balaenoptera is a compound of the Latin word *balaena* (= whale) and the Greek word *pteron* (= wing, that is, horn). *Musculus* is believed to be either derived from the Latin word *musculus* (= muscle) or a diminutive of the Latin word *mus* (= mouse (*musculus* = the little mouse)), in which case the name was originally conceived as a joke; the muscle-mound with the dorsal fin or the little mouse with the dorsal fin.

blue whale
Balaenoptera musculus

MORE INFORMATION ON PAGE 90

id checklist

BODY: Unusually long. Grey-black on top, white underneath. Clear divisions between coloured areas on sides. Asymmetrical spots on sides of head, with the right jaw being light-yellow or white and the left jaw being black. The head is tapered and sharp at the end and has a peculiar crest. The tail stock is slender, even thin on the sides.

DORSAL FIN: Relatively high, about 60 cm, either triangular or crescent-shaped.

FLIPPERS: Long and narrow.

FLUKES: Broad, although delicate, with a notch in the middle. Flukes, generally submerged, are hidden from view.

DIVING: Commonest dive lasts 5 to 15 minutes, but can be longer; whale capable of reaching a depth of 230 m.

BLOWING: Column high and narrow, reaching a height of 4 to 6 m; can be seen from a considerable distance. Dorsal fin discernible almost immediately after the blow. Snout emerges first when whale breaks surface.

SWIMMING: Often swims slowly, but can reach 30 km per hour, if necessary.

HABITAT: Sometimes near land, but primarily a whale of the open ocean; preferred depth is 400 to 1,200 m.

NATURE: Not wary of ships; sometimes breaches.

Order:	Whales (*Cetacea*), 78 species.
Suborder:	Baleen whales (*Mysticeti*), 10 species.
Superfamily:	[None.]
Family:	Rorquals (*Balaenopteridae*), 6 species.
Subfamily:	*Balaenopterinae*, 5 species.
Genus:	*Balaenoptera*, 5 species.
Species:	*B. physalus*.

Length/weight (newborn):	6-6.5 m / 1.5-2 tons.
Length (adult):	♀ 19.5-27 m. ♂ 18-25 m.
Weight (adult):	♀ 50-100 tons. ♂ 30-80 tons.
Lifetime:	100 years.
World population:	120,000-150,000.
In Icelandic waters:	9,000-10,000.
Group size:	1, 2-10(30).
Diet:	

Balaenoptera physalus (Linnaeus, 1758).
Synonym: *Balaena antipodarum, Balaena boops, Balaena antiquorum, Balaena tschudii, Balaena boops, Balaena mysticetus major, Balaena physalis, Balaena physalus, Balaena quoyi, Balaena rostrata australis, Balaena rostrata major, Balaena sulcata, Balaena sulcata arctica, Balaenoptera antarctica, Balaenoptera aragous, Balaenoptera australis, Balaenoptera blythii, Balaenoptera brasiliensis, Balaenoptera gibbar, Balaenoptera mediterraneensis, Balaenoptera mediterranensis, Balaenoptera musculus, Balaenoptera paragonica, Balaenoptera patachonica, Balaenoptera patachonicus, Balaenoptera physalus physalus, Balaenoptera physalus quoyi, Balaenoptera physalus quoyii, Balaenoptera quoyii, Balaenoptera rorqual, Balaenoptera swinhoei, Balaenoptera swinhoii, Balaenoptera tenuirostris, Balaenoptera tschudii, Balaenoptera velifera, Balaenoptera velifera copei, Balaenopteris guibusdam, Benedenia knoxii, Dubertus rhodinsulensis, Physalis vulgaris, Physalus antarcticus, Physalus australis, Physalus brasiliensis, Physalus duguidii, Physalus fasciatus, Physalus patachonicus, Physalus verus, Pterobalaena communis, Pterobalaena gigantea michrochira, Rorqualus musculus, Sibbaldius tectirostris, Sibbaldius tuberosus, Stenobalaena xanthogaster, Swinhoia chinensis.*

 Langreyður. Langareyður; finnhvalur; fiskreki; sildreki; steypireyður.

 Finnkval. Langrør; loddekval; rørkval; sildekval; silderør.

 Rorcual comun. Ballena; ballena boba; ballena de aleta; bramuna; fisalo; músculo; rorcual; rorcual commún; rorcual comun; rorcual común.

 Balenottera comune. Capidolio.

 Finnwal. Finnfisch; Gemeiner Finnwal.

 Rorqual commun. Baleine de Saint-Cyprien; baleine Gibbar; poisson de Jupiter; rorqual de la Méditerranée; vraie baleine.

Fin whale. Bastard whale; common finback; common finback whale; common finwhale; common rorqual; finback; finback whale; fin fish; finfish; finnback; finner; finner whale; fin-whale; gibbar; great northern rorqual; herring whale; jupiter fish; Orkney whale; razor back; razorback; razorback whale; round-lipped whale.

Balaenoptera is a compound of the Latin word *balaena* (= whale), derived from the Greek work *phallaena* (= whale) and the Greek word *pteron* (= wing, that is, horn). Physalus is believed to originate from the Greek words *physis* (=essence; nature) and *alos* (= sea) and/or from *phusalis* (= inflated musical instrument), reference to the hunting method of this family. Along the way, the Greek word *physalos* acquires the meaning of rorqual; *the rorqual with the dorsal fin or the inflated whale with the dorsal fin.*

fin whale
Balaenoptera physalus

Distribution

id *checklist*

BODY: Long and slender although not as thin as the fin whale's body, and the sei whale's head is rounder. Dark-grey or black on back, tail stock and flippers, but light-coloured on underbelly. Both sides of head, viewed from above, are equally dark. Light-coloured patches dispersed on body and flecks on head. An upright band or narrow comb runs from blowhole almost to end of snout.

DORSAL FIN: About 60 cm, very erect and crescent-shaped, situated toward front of animal.

FLIPPERS: Slender and proportionally short (about 10% of animal's total weight).

FLUKES: Triangular; notch in middle.

DIVING: For 5 to 20 minutes.

BLOWING: Small, expanding column, reaching up 3 m at most.

SWIMMING: Usually near surface, rather slow swimmer going 2 to 6.5 km per hour while hunting food; 5 to 14 km per hour on long journeys. Capable, however, of reaching speeds of 30+ km per hour. Not much of animal is visible on surface, the tail stock and flukes, for example, not being lifted out of water. Blowhole and dorsal fin, however, both visible at same time.

HABITAT: An open-ocean whale; preferred depth is 500 to 1,300 m.

NATURE: Known to breach, coming out of water at a low angle, never going high.

Order:	Whales (Cetacea), 78 species.
Suborder:	Baleen whales (Mysticeti), 10 species.
Superfamily:	[None.]
Family:	Rorquals (Balaenopteridae), 6 species.
Subfamily:	Balaenopterinae, 5 species.
Genus:	Balaenoptera, 5 species.
Species:	B. borealis.

Length/weight (newborn):	4.4-4.8 m / 725-780 kg.
Length (adult):	♀ 14.5-21 m. ♂ 12-20 m.
Weight (adult):	♀ 25-30 tons. ♂ 20-25 tons.
Lifetime:	80 years.
World population:	50,000-70,000.
In Icelandic waters:	10,500.
Group size:	1, 2-5(30).
Diet:	

Balaenoptera borealis (Lesson, 1828).
Synonym: *Balaena rostrata, Balaenoptera alba, Balaenoptera arctica, Balaenoptera borealis borealis, Balaenoptera borealis schlegelii, Balaenoptera iwasi, Balaenoptera laticeps, Balaenoptera schlegeli, Balaenoptera schlegelii, Balaenoptera schlegelii, Pterobalaena alba, Pterobalaena schlegeli alba, Sibbaldius alba, Sibbaldius schlegelii, Sibbaldus borealis, Sibbaldus schlegelii.*

 Sandreyður. Bísill; geirreyður; katthveli; sæhvalur.

 Seikval. Sei.

 Rorcual norteno. Ballena boba; ballena boreal; rorcual de garganta rosada; rorcual de Rudolphi; rorcual mediano; rorcual norteño.

 Balenottera boreale. Balenattera artica.

Seiwal. Rudolphi's Finnwal; Rudolphis Finnwal.

Rorqual de Rudolphi. Baleine d'Ostende; baleine noir; baleinoptère boréal; baleinoptère d'Ostende; rorqual boréal; rorqual de Rudolph; rorqual du Nord.

Sei whale. Coal-fish whale; coalfish whale; cod-whale; great northern rorqual; flat-back; Japan finner; Ostend whale; pollack whale; Rudolph's rorqual; Rudolphi's rorqual; sardine whale; sei; siegval; walfish whale.

Balaenoptera is a compound of the Latin word *balaena* (= whale) and the Greek word *pteron* (= wing, that is, horn). *Borealis* is Latin (= northerly; from the North); the whale from the North with the dorsal fin.

sei whale
Balaenoptera borealis

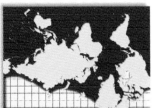

id checklist

BODY: Generally black or dark-grey on back and sides.

DORSAL FIN: Relatively high, curved slightly aft (crescent-shaped).

FLIPPERS: Rather long and narrow, often with a white streak or belt running across breadth.

FLUKES: Large and broad. However, usually not lifted out of water when animal dives.

DIVING: Usually lasts 3 to 8 minutes, although up to 20 minutes is possible. The snout appears first when the whale resurfaces.

BLOWING: Column is generally 2 to 3 m high, spherical and hazy, so visible only in best weather conditions.

SWIMMING: Powerful swimmer, generally fast. Blowhole and dorsal fin are visible at the same time.

HABITAT: Primarily a whale of the shallows although it can also be seen in deeper waters; preferred depth is 50 to 400 m.

NATURE: Unlike other rorqual whales, can be very curious, especially young animals, often approaching ships and boats. Often very sportive. Known to emerge from the water at a 45° angle and breach high into the air, re-entering water head-first; rakish and nimble like a dolphin. Also comes down on side or back like the humpback whale, with accompanying splashing and noise.

Order:	Whales (Cetacea), 78 species.
Suborder:	Baleen whales (Mysticeti), 10 species.
Superfamily:	[None.]
Family:	Rorquals (Balaenopteridae), 6 species.
Subfamily:	Balaenopterinae, 5 species.
Genus:	Balaenoptera, 5 species.
Species:	B. acutorostrata.
Subspecies:	B. a. acutorostrata, B. a. bonarensis and B. a. davidsonii.

Length/weight (newborn):	2.4-2.84 m / 350-400 kg.
Length (adult):	♀ 8.5-11 m. ♂ 7-9.8 m.
Weight (adult):	♀ 8-10 tons. ♂ 5-8 tons.
Lifetime:	50 years.
World population:	1,000,000.
In Icelandic waters:	55,000.
Group size:	1, 2-3(40).
Diet:	

Balaenoptera acutorostrata (Lacépède, 1804).
Synonym: Agaphelus gibbosus, Balaena gibbosa, Balaena microcephala, Balaena minima, Balaena minimus borealis, Balaena rostrata, Balaenoptera acutorostrata bonarensis, Balaenoptera acutorostrata davidsoni, Balaenoptera acutorostrata thalmaha, Balaenoptera bonarensis, Balaenoptera dactylaena huttoni, Balaenoptera davidsoni, Balaenoptera eschrichtii, Balaenoptera huttoni, Balaenoptera longimana, Balaenoptera microcephala, Balaenoptera racovitzai, Balaenoptera rostrata, Neobalaena marginata, Physalus antarcticus, Pterobalaena minor, Pterobalaena minor bergensis, Pterobalaena minor groenlandica, Pterobalaena nana pentadactyla, Pterobalaena nana tetradactyla, Pterobalaena pentadactyla, Rorqualus boops, Rorqualus minor, Sibbaldius mondinii, Sibbaldus mondinii.

 Hrafnreyður. Dettir; hnýfill; hrafnhvalur; HREFNA; léttir; sildarhnýfill; snefja; stökkull.

 Vågekval. Minke; minkekval.

Rorcual aliblanco. Ballena de rostro agudo; ballena enana; ballena pequeña; ballenato; rorcual menor.

Balenottera minore. Balenottera rostrata.

Zwergwal. Hechtwal; Schnabelwal; Sild; Sommerwal; Zwergfinnfisch.

Petit rorqual. Baleine à bec; baleine d'été; baleine naine; baleinoptère rostré; rorqual à museau pointu; rorqual à rostre; rorqual musseau-pointu; souffleur.

 Minke whale. Bagwhale; bay whale; beaked whale; fin-backed whale; least rorqual; lesser finback; lesser finner; lesser fin whale; lesser rorqual; little finner; little mink; little piked whale; minke; minkie; pike-whale; pike whale; piked whale; pikehead; pikehead whale; pikewhale; sharp-headed finner; sharpheaded finner; sharp-headed finner whale; sharp-nosed finner; short whalebone whale; smaller rorqual; sprat whale; summer whale; young finback.

Balaenoptera is a compound of the Latin word balaena (= whale) and the Greek word pteron (= wing, that is, horn). Acutorostrata is a compound of the Latin word acutus (= sharp; narrow-pointed; acute) and rostrum (= nose; muzzle; snout); the narrow-nosed whale with the dorsal fin.

minke whale
Balaenoptera acutorostrata

beluga whale
Delphinapterus leucas

The beluga whale belongs to the sub-order of toothed whales (*Odontoceti*), the superfamily of dolphins (*Delphinoidea*) and the family of white whales (*Monodontidae*) along with the narwhal. Then, it is in the subfamily *Delphinapterinae* and finally in the genus *Delphinapterus*, of which it is the sole member.

An adult beluga whale is usually completely white, 3 to 5 m long, and 400 to 1,500 kg, depending on the stock to which it belongs. Males are usually bigger than females. The head and mouth are small and abrupt. The mouth has 36 to 40 small, cone-shaped teeth. There is no dorsal fin, which is believed to have been lost in adaptation as unsuitable for the whale's swimming under ice. The beluga whale is exclusively a coldwater whale with an extensive distribution in the oceans of the North Pole, although not in deep waters. Its numbers are great along the west coast of Greenland, around Svalbard and along the coast of Siberia.

Despite its predisposition to cold seas, the beluga whale also journeys occasionally far to the South, especially in hard times when the polar seas are glaciated. The whale often stays near the shore and even in shallows, being one of the few species of whale that enters the mouths of large rivers in the colder reaches. There, the beluga whale

The polar bear is one of the beluga whale's natural enemies.

is mostly hunting salmon. Thus, the whale frequents the Gulf of St. Lawrence in Canada and the Yukon River in Alaska. There the whale has been known to go as far as 1,000 km upriver. In the same way, the beluga whale goes up the Yenisei and Amur rivers in Siberia. On these forced journeys to escape the cold and ice of the polar seas, the beluga whale sometimes goes to Iceland and south along the coast of Norway, into the North Sea and even into the Baltic Sea.

The beluga whale eats every kind of fish, for example salmon, and also takes squid and octopus, or anything else it finds and can handle, including bottom animals and krill. How deep the beluga whale dives, on average, is not known, but it has been said that scientists once were able to train an animal to descend to 650 m and remain there for 15 minutes.

Experts believe it unlikely that the beluga whale has to search so deep as a rule since, as was mentioned above, it is mostly a whale of the shallows. Most people agree that its food is usually fished in shallower seas, somewhere between the surface and a depth of 300 m at the most.

The beluga whale is extremely gregarious, often forming groups of 1,000 or more animals.

Experts believe female beluga whales mature sexually at about five years of age, while the males take three years longer, reaching sexual maturity at eight. Mating occurs when the ice starts to melt, and pregnancy lasts 14 months, with births coming in the spring or summer. The females then stay in secluded fjords or along the shoreline to give birth. Newborn calves are about 1.5 m long, weighing about 80 kg. They are dark-coloured at first, that is, brownish or greyish. This changes after two years to a bluer tone, lightening over time until at 5 to 12 years of age, they become snow-white.

The beluga whale is known for producing many, beautiful high-frequency sounds. These phenomenal tones are most reminiscent of birdsong. The whale is sometimes dubbed the "canary whale" in other languages. To produce these sounds, the beluga whale seems to use the dome of its forehead as a sounding board, for people have noted its shape changing, depending on what sounds are being emitted. No other whale is thought to have command over such diverse sounds. It now seems clear that a complex language of signals is involved.

Another remarkable thing about the beluga whale, and, in fact, also about the narwhal, is the peculiar and actually unique ability to turn its head up, down and to both sides. The reason for this mobility is that the neck joints are not fused as they are in other whale species. In addition, the beluga whale can move its flippers more freely than whales commonly do and can even use them to swim backward. The whale also has labial mobility, being able to alter the shape of its mouth, even to a pucker.

To endure the great cold that undeniably is the animal's lot, living as far north as it does, the beluga whale has an unusually thick skin and a great layer of blubber. This makes the whale very desirable prey for the Inuits of Greenland who utilise it for food. The beluga is actually their most prized whale and has undoubtedly been so for all Eskimos in the countries of the North from time immemorial. These days, the animals are usually shot with a rifle close to holes in the ice. Then, they are harpooned before they sink and are lost. The average annual catch has been 400 to 1,000 animals. In addition to the Eskimos, larger nations have also hewn briskly into the world stocks of beluga whale. They have especially coveted the thick leather or hide of this whale, which, for a long time, was used in the manufacture of boots and lacing. In addition, the oil, meat and blubber were utilised. In 1871, Norwegians caught more than 2,000 animals off Svalbard and Novaja Semlja. Over the 37-year period from 1874 to 1911, Scottish whalers took about 11,000 animals in Elwin Bay in Somerset Island in the polar region of Canada. And the average catch of the Soviets from 1900 to 1960 was 3,000 to 4,000 animals per year.

Today, little whaling of the beluga is done. However, individual stocks are deemed to be possibly at risk.

The beluga whale has, however, other enemies. One is the killer whale, which the beluga whale fears greatly. The salmon fishermen of Alaska have played unsparingly on this fear when the beluga whale has swum up rivers in the spring and summer after salmon. The fishermen only have to play a tape of the killer whale's intra-group calls, and the beluga whale flees.

Mostly, the beluga whale seeks protection in the drift ice since the killer whale cannot manoeuvre there because of its dorsal fin.

Polar bears are also said to be an enemy of the beluga whale. They catch the whale the same way as the Inuits of Greenland do, that is, through a quickly shrinking air hole in the ice when the weather is extremely cold and harsh.

Another way is to find a whale stranded in shallows. It is thought that even walruses sometimes kill these ocean singers.

Yet another enemy has been added to this group in recent years. It is the quickly growing pollution from all kinds of waste substances, not to mention frequent oil spills. These often hew savagely into the marine biosphere. Today, 50,000 to 70,000 animals survive worldwide, according to scientists' best estimates.

The beluga whale was the first whale species people hunted for the sole purpose of exhibiting them alive in pens. This was done in England in 1877. The animal came from Labrador and, then, another one a year later. This species of whale can still be seen today in many aquariums all over the world.

narwhal
Monodon monoceros

The narwhal belongs to the suborder of toothed whales (Odontoceti), the superfamily of dolphins (Delphinoidea), and the family of Monodontidae, along with the beluga whale.

Then, it is in the subfamily Monodontinae and finally in the genus Monodon, of which it is the sole member.

The narwhal is, on average, 3.5 to 5 m long and weighs 800 to 1,600 kg. The males are larger than the females.

Like the beluga whale, the narwhal has no dorsal fin. Its flippers are short, flaring out a bit at the tips as the whale matures. The flukes are a different shape than is found on other whales. They most resemble a fan, gathered in the middle.

The head is small and bulbous, the snout barely distinguishable and the mouth small.

To put it mildly, the narwhal has few teeth, actually only two. One is on the left side of the upper jaw, near the front, and the other on the right side, both about 20 cm long. However, when the male grows older and matures, the left tooth suddenly begins to grow straight out from the head with an anti-clockwise twist (from the whale's perspective). It can grow to 20 cm in diameter, weighing some 10 kg, and reach a length of 3 m in old animals, which is more than half the length of the body. Then, we are actually talking about a 7- to 8-m beast instead of one of 3.5 to 5 m, as previously mentioned. Customarily, though, the tusk is not considered when the length is calculated, that is, only the length between the snout and the flukes is measured. There is no enamel on the tusk. Rather, the substance is similar to ivory. The females do not have a tusk,

except in exceptional instances. On the other hand, it sometimes happens that the right tooth in males also starts to grow out, parallel to the left one. This occurrence is rare, being some form of aberration. The right tusk is always smaller.

The narwhal's colour varies, depending on its age. The calves are born dark-grey or bluish and then darken, becoming black in their adolescence. However, when they approach sexual maturity, the animals begin to take on a lighter colour, first on their underbelly. They later take on a dappled or pied pattern, which is unique among whales. The dark colouring also changes to a greener tone. Very mature animals become almost totally white, especially males. It is commonly thought that the whale's name, which is very ancient, originated because of this white-mottled colouring that could resemble a corpse (the Icelandic word for narwhal

The long, twisted tusk of the narwhal has always been regarded as a remarkable thing, and early on became an object of desire. In 1111, for example, Sigurdur, Sojourner to Jerusalem, presented the Emperor of Constantinople with such a tusk, and in 1621, the Bishop in Hólar, Gudbrandur Thorláksson, sent another to the Danish King, Christian IV.

When increased numbers of narwhal tusks began to appear in mainland Europe and even in China, many believed they were the horn of the mythical unicorn. The unicorn was first mentioned in European treatises in about 400 BC,

is náhvalur from nár (=corpse) and hvalur (=whale)) that had been in the sea a long time.

Others associate the name with the Old German "narwa", related to the English word

more precisely in the book Indika by the Greek, Ktesias. The animal's habitat was supposed to be India.

The unicorn was often drawn like a horse, but with the hindlegs of an antelope and the tail of a lion. People believed that the horn, which was in the middle of the forehead, was imbued with supernatural power that was effective against poison and various diseases, such as impotency. It is not surprising that people aspired to own such things. Even foreign bishops coveted them and used them in their crosiers.

The truth was not made known to the world until 1638 when Ole Worm, a professor of medicine at the University of Copenhagen, wrote a scholarly article on the matter. Even into the 19th century, rumours were heard that unicorns truly existed and were in good health. They were supposedly spotted in either Africa or the Tibetan highlands.

Nowadays, the unicorn is perhaps most familiar in the coat of arms of the British Crown, where it symbolises Scotland.

"narrow", taking the tusk as the name's origin.

The narwhal is distributed throughout the oceans surrounding the North Pole and is one of the most northerly and

cold-tolerant animals in the world. It generally frequents the edge of the polar ice, even to the north of Greenland and Franz Josef Land. It has been known to swim far beneath the ice. In the autumn, when it begins to get colder, the whale is unwilling to depart from there, often gathering under air holes. Sometimes they get frozen in there and die.

The narwhal is not as willing to approach coastlines as its relative, the beluga whale, and usually prefers to stay rather far from land. They are generally in small groups of from 2 to 20 animals. Larger shoals of 1,000 or more animals can be found, which then are subdivided into smaller units, that is, of males, females with new-born calves, etc.

The narwhal's main diet is fish, such as cod and various flat fish, but also squid, octopus, shrimp and even smaller animals like krill and other crustaceans. No one knows how deep the narwhal dives for its prey, but several hundred metres is considered likely. Generally, though, the whale stays down only 7 to 20 minutes at a time. Because the narwhal has so few teeth, experts think it likely that it uses some kind of suction method of gathering its food, similar to what the walrus does to cope with the same "problem".

The narwhal migrates south in the spring to mate, and the next summer, after 14 to 15 months, the females give birth. Then, the animals are usually in distant, deep fjords in Northern Canada, North Greenland and Northern Norway. A newborn calf is about 160 cm long and weighs around 80 kg. It nurses for one year or even longer. Experts think that the females mature sexually at 4 to 7 years of age and bear young every three years. Males, on the other hand, do not mature sexually until they are 8 to 13 years old.

One mystery has puzzled scientists for a long time. How does the narwhal employ its twisted, gigantic tusk? Various explanations have been offered, for example, that the animal uses it to spear fish or to break an air hole in the ice, or that it lays the tusk up on the ice edge to make it easier to stay afloat during rest or sleep. Another idea is that the whale uses the tusk as some kind of antenna or rather a transmitter, with sounds being focused into one point at the tip of the tusk.

However, since the tusk is generally found in male animals only, it seems clear that it must be related in some way to gender. One might therefore suppose that the tusk was only a sexual emblem and conceivably also a sceptre, as, for example, for various deer, where the most vigorous and strongest males have the biggest horns. Scientists had reports from whalers in the past of, and have many times witnessed, fencing bouts between narwhals (if this is the appropriate term). They rub their tusks together as if to appraise their relative strength.

There are also instances of narwhals being found dead, with shallow wounds and scars in their heads from such a tusk, as if from a battle. However, the tusk is hollow, not solid, as one might have expected.

It may be that narwhals wield this tusk for some other purpose as well, and that the above-mentioned conjectures have some basis in logic. The same can be said for running the tusk along a silty bottom to flush prey, as divers who were laying oil pipelines once saw, and to which the polished point also attests. However, it seems clear that the males are in no way dependent on their tusk to get food.

Inuits have traditionally utilised this whale species for food, both in Greenland and in the polar regions of Canada. The tusk understandably has not reduced their interest since it is a popular commodity. About 1,000 animals are caught annually in these areas. In practice, this means about 4,000 are killed because only one of every four animals shot is brought in; the rest sink and are lost. Statistics from other places are not known.

Other enemies of the narwhal are killer whales and polar bears. Perhaps walruses, if threatened, also kill narwhals. Experts believe that the shark does not attack living animals, but rather feeds on their carcasses.

Annals tell of some narwhals that washed up on the shores of Iceland long ago. This, in fact, still happens today. At the end of the last century, for example, a narwhal washed up on the coast below Reykhólar in Eastern Bardaströnd County. The tusk was taken and later given to Magnús Stephensen who was then a powerful Icelander and a representative of the Danish king. Then, in 1976 two narwhals washed ashore in Geldinganes close to Reykjavík.

Several attempts have been made to transport narwhals to aquariums, but they have mostly been failures; the animals have generally died within four months.

harbour porpoise
Phocoena phocoena

The harbour porpoise belongs to the suborder of toothed whales (*Odontoceti*) and the superfamily of dolphins (*Delphinoidea*). It was once classified to the family *Delphinidae*. However, after further research on marine mammals, scientists realised that despite similarities to this family, a very different animal was involved, regarding both appearance and behaviour. A new family, *Phocoenidae*, was therefore established for the relevant species of the speckled porpoise (*Australophoecaena dioptrica*), Dall's porpoise (*Phocoenoides dalli*), vaquita (*Phocoena sinus*), Burmeister's porpoise (*Phocoena spinipinnis*), the finless porpoise (*Neophocaena phocaenoides*) and the harbour porpoise (*Phocoena phocoena*). This last is the only member of its family in the North Atlantic. It is also the smallest toothed whale found off Iceland's coast, while probably being, at the same time, the whale species Icelanders get to know first. The harbour porpoise is of the subfamily *Phocoeninae*, to distinguish it from the porpoises with a pronounced black-and-white coloration. Finally, the harbour porpoise is in the genus *Phocoena*.

The harbour porpoise can vary in colour, but is generally dark-grey on the top, tail stock and flippers, but lighter on the sides and underbelly. Like other species in the family, the harbour porpoise has a very rakish build, nearly perfectly streamlined, most resembling tuna. It is one of the smallest whales, being only 160 cm long, on average, and weighing about 50 kg. Females are a bit smaller than males.

The porpoise's head is small and its snout abrupt. Its dorsal fin is rather low and rounded at the top. It has small flippers and flukes. In addition, the tail stock is very thin and seemingly weak, compared with other porpoises. The teeth number between 40 and 60 in each jaw. They are relatively small and, unique to this superfamily, spatulate, perfect for snipping prey to pieces.

The harbour porpoise is primarily a whale of the shallows, its principal habitation being the Northern Hemisphere in both the Atlantic and the Pacific Oceans. It is found from the Gulf of Alaska south to California on the West Coast of the United States. Then, harbour porpoise distribution runs from the Gulf of St. Lawrence south to Cape Delaware on the South Carolina shore on the East Coast of the United States. Harbour porpoises also are off the West Coast of Greenland from the Davis Strait east to Scoresbysund. There is another belt from Iceland to the Faeroe Islands and from there to the Norwegian coast and then from the Kara Sea in the North to West Africa,

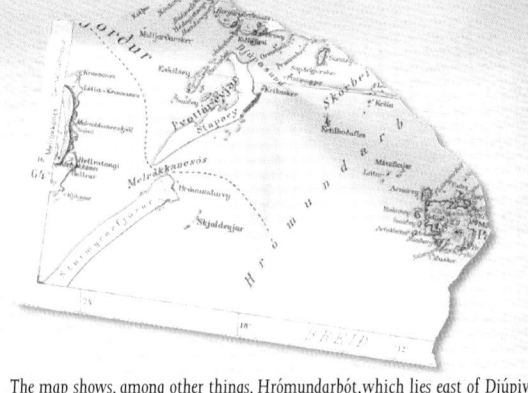

The map shows, among other things, Hrómundarbót, which lies east of Djúpivogur. There, four men in a boat from Hamarsfjordur caught more than 30 harbour porpoises in one day at the beginning of this century. They had to string some of the catch together to bring it in.

touching the Mediterranean Sea. There is also an isolated harbour porpoise stock in the Black Sea. Finally, another area lies from the Kamchatka Peninsula in the North and south almost to Japan. The harbour porpoise is migratory, that is, it seeks out warmer waters in the winter, but comes to Iceland in the early spring, especially to the southern coast and Faxaflói Bay, hunting herring and capelin shoals. It then travels along the coast into bays and fjords and is very common in shallows and even in estuaries. In this respect, the harbour porpoise is unlike most other whales. It gets its food along the ocean bottom.

Harbour porpoises are generally in pods of a few, travelling relatively inconspicuously. Most commonly, 2 to 10 animals will be seen, although larger shoals of up to 250 animals or more have been observed. Unlike dolphins, they very seldom leap out of the water.

Pregnancy takes about 11 months, with calves most likely being born in the summer. Females, believed to mature sexually at three years of age, bear young annually. Males mature sexually several years later than females.

Previously, some hunting of harbour porpoise was done off Iceland, especially for food supplies in the spring. This was done mostly in Breidafjordur and the West Fjords, but also became common in many other places. For centuries the animals were harpooned until better fishing equipment was found. Then, when shotguns and nets came along, they were also utilised, and a considerable quantity of harbour porpoise was often caught. From early in this century, for example, there is an

account of four people in a boat in Hamarsfjordur who got 30 harbour porpoises in one day in the area known as Hrómundarbót, west of Papey Island. They had to string some of the catch together to bring it to land. It was considered great sport to shoot this whale, and there were several famous porpoise shooters from Berufjordur and Hamarsfjordur. The art entailed shooting the animals at precisely the right moment when they had just filled their lungs and were about to dive deep.

After cod nets came into use, a considerable number of harbour porpoises always got tangled in them and were utilised. An old farmer in Berufjordur, for example, remembers having set 15 to 20 cod nets in Reydarskersbót off Berufjordur in about 1950. 16 harbour porpoises were caught in them.

Nowadays, there is no organ-

ised hunting of the harbour porpoise in Iceland, at least not on a large scale. However, people sometimes take one harbour porpoise at a time. Other nations catch the harbour porpoise, for example, off the coast of Washington State in the United States as well as in Canada and Greenland, the Sea of Azov and the Black Sea. Greenlanders are believed to catch the most harbour porpoise, 1,500 animals per year.

Nothing is known of the size of the stock. However, it seems clear that the number of harbour porpoises is rapidly decreasing, not least because the ocean areas it relies on for its sustenance are becoming polluted.

People have tried to put this little porpoise in aquariums and train it, but this has not been very successful.

white-beaked dolphin
Lagenorhynchus albirostris

 The white-beaked dolphin belongs to the suborder of toothed whales (Odontoceti), the superfamily Delphinoidea and the family of Delphinidae. This is the most diverse whale family, with 31 species altogether. It is also in the subfamily Delphininae and finally in the genus of Lagenorhynchus.

The white-beaked dolphin is so robust that it could be called a mound of muscle, but it is nevertheless very rakish and streamlined. Fully grown, it is about 2.5 to 3 m long, weighing around 180 kg. Males are a bit larger than females.

The dorsal fin, located halfway between the snout and flukes, is relatively high and pointed, especially on males, with the top curving slightly back. The

flippers are rather long and wide, becoming pointed at the ends. The snout is short and thick, but quite defined. It is generally white, although it can also be brownish or greyish. In each jaw, there are 42 to 56 teeth, the fewest found in any member of the dolphin family.

The white-beaked dolphin's colouring is otherwise singular and even variable from one animal to another. Still, for the most part, the colouring is dark on the upper part of the body and white on the lower part. In other places on the body, grey, black and white blend in a complex pattern that, however, is not always clearly partitioned. One of the best identifying marks is a light-grey patch in back of the dorsal fin on each side of the tail stock.

Of any of the dolphins found off Iceland, the least is known of the white-beaked dolphin, even though it is believed to be the most common species. White-beaked dolphins generally travel in small groups, it being most common to see 10 to 100 at once. Larger schools of 1,000 animals, however, occur, but are rather rare.

The white-beaked dolphin is a migratory whale and also the species of small dolphin ranging farthest north. Its home base is in the coldest waters of the North Atlantic, as far north as Murmansk on the Kola Peninsula in Russia and Scoresbysund in Greenland and from there over to the West Coast on the same parallel. These whales are therefore in the southernmost part of the Barents Sea, in the Norwegian Sea, the North Sea, in parts of the Baltic Sea and as far south as the British Isles, and even in the Bay of Biscay. From there, its distribution reaches to the Faeroe Islands, Iceland and both sides of the tip of Greenland, that is from the Greenland Sea around to the Davis Strait.

In 1991, this white-beaked dolphin got caught in a net south of Iceland and drowned. It proved to be 3 m long and weighed 370 kg, which is 100 kg more than books say is the maximum weight.

In addition, white-beaked dolphins are along the coast of Labrador, around Newfoundland and off Nova Scotia, even reaching the shores of Massachusetts in the United States. The knowledge of mating habits and pregnancy, as is true of many other things regarding this species of dolphin, is very limited. Specialists believe that mating takes place in the spring or summer, and that the term of pregnancy is 10-12 months. The mainstay of the dolphin's diet is diverse. It includes various schooling species of fish, for example, cod, herring and capelin, in addition to squid, octopus and crustaceans. White-beaked dolphins are often seen in the company of fin whales in the Greenland Sea when both are after capelin.

Distinguishing the white-beaked dolphin from the Atlantic white-sided dolphin is often difficult in the ocean because they are very similar. Therefore, dolphins classed as white-beaked dolphins in surveys could just as well be the latter species. It is, however, clear that there is a considerable number of white-beaked dolphins off Iceland. This inference can be made from the frequency with which white-beaked dolphins are found beached here. In fact, such finds are more frequent in Iceland than for any other whale species.

After whale surveys in 1987 and 1989, a rough estimate of the total number of white-beaked dolphins in the ocean around Iceland is 12,000 to 20,000 animals. The world population, however, is completely unknown, although believed to be a few hundred thousand animals.

Through the years, the white-beaked dolphin has not been hunted for profit except on a small scale. Some were taken years ago in the fjords of Northern Norway. There are also references to the Faeroese's having fished a few hundred animals at the beginning of this century, although it is not completely clear whether these were white-beaked dolphins or Atlantic white-sided dolphins or a mixture of the two. Some have also been killed off Greenland, and recent research in Labrador indicates that fishermen there catch, on average, about 400 white-beaked dolphins annually. Off Iceland, and, in fact, elsewhere, white-beaked dolphins have, on occasion, got tangled in nets and died. If possible, they are utilised.

atlantic white sided dolphin

Lagenorhynchus acutus

 The Atlantic white-sided dolphin belongs to the suborder of toothed whales (*Odontoceti*), the super-family of dolphins (*Delphinoidea*) and the family of *Delphinidae*, the most numerous family of whales, having 31 species altogether. The Atlantic white-sided dolphin is also in the subfamily of small dolphins (*Delphininae*) and finally in the genus *Lagenorhynchus*.

This dolphin greatly resembles the closely related species of white-beaked dolphin. The Atlantic white-sided dolphin is very strongly built and also extremely rakish and beautiful to behold. It is, however, a bit smaller than the white-beaked dolphin, about 2 to 2.5 m long and weighing about 165 kg. Males are larger than females.

The Atlantic white-sided dolphin has unique coloration: black on the upper body and flippers, grey on the sides and white on the underbelly. In addition, there is a yellow-green or bright yellow oblong patch on each side, that is, on the boundaries of the black and grey colours, behind the dorsal fin. There is also a white patch a little closer to the head. It would not be out of place to say that the colour pattern was complex, but clear-cut.

The dorsal fin is in the centre, relatively high and sharply pointed, especially on the males, the top sweeping slightly back. The flippers are rather long and broad at the base, but narrow sharply at the ends. The tail stock is extremely thick and large and virtually solid muscle.

The shape of the snout resembles that of the white-beaked dolphin, that is, relatively short and knobby, black on top and white underneath. The whale has 58 to 80 teeth in each jaw. Experts believe that the Atlantic white-sided dolphin is a migratory whale, as is common with dolphins. However, little is known of its migratory routes. It is generally in groups of a few, the commonest size ranging from 10 to100. Larger schools of over 1,000 animals are rather rare, but have been observed. There seems to be a definite division or composition of groups among the animals, especially as to age. Thus, it seems that young, immature animals keep away from mixed groups comprising females, their new-born offspring and several males.

Experts believe that Atlantic white-sided dolphins mature sexually at 6 to 12 years of age. Based on very limited knowledge, experts believe that mating and birth occur in the spring or summer, and that pregnancy lasts 10 to 12 months. New-born calves are about 120 cm long and weigh approximately 40 kg. They nurse for an estimated 18 months.

The females are thought to give birth every two to three years.

The Atlantic white-sided dolphin, unlike most of our other dolphin species, prefers the high seas. This is one of the reasons why it is very seldom found washed up on beaches. In fact, only two instances of such occurrences are known. It must also be kept in mind how difficult it is distinguishing between the white-beaked dolphin and the Atlantic white-sided dolphin in the field, due to their similarity. People especially try to use the colour pattern for identification and the dorsal fin, which is sharper and more curved on the Atlantic white-sided dolphin than on the white-beaked dolphin. Also, the distribution of the Atlantic white-sided dolphin is the same as for the white-beaked dolphin, that is, the northern reaches of the North Atlantic. The northernmost boundaries are, on the one hand, Nuuk on the West Coast of Greenland and, on the other, Trondheim in Norway. The southernmost boundaries are Cape Cod on the East Coast of the United States and the British Isles.

Nevertheless, Atlantic white-sided dolphins have been spotted outside these boundaries, both farther north in the Barents Sea and farther south near France.

The Atlantic white-sided dolphin's diet is diverse: small schooling fish like herring, mackerel and sand lance as well as squid and octopus.

There is no record through the ages of the Atlantic white-sided dolphin's being systematically killed in any quantity, as was common with larger whales. This, however, happened sometimes, although episodically. In the 19th century, on at least two occasions, more than 2,000 animals were killed near Bergen, Norway, but nowadays, there is a totally different atmosphere there.

Elsewhere, some animals are taken, for example, in the Faeroe Islands, where in 1988, 600 animals were driven onto land and killed. This is actually an unusually high figure. Also, off the south and west coasts of Greenland and the south-eastern coast of Canada, some Atlantic white-sided dolphins, along with other small dolphin species, sometimes get tangled in fishing nets and are killed.

common dolphin
Delphinus delphis

The common dolphin belongs to the suborder of toothed whales (*Odontoceti*), the superfamily of dolphins (*Delphinoidea*) and the family of *Delphinidae*, the most numerous family of whales, having 31 species altogether. The common dolphin is classified to the subfamily of small dolphins (*Delphininae*) and, finally, to the genus *Delphinus*, of which it is the sole member.

The common dolphin, being 1.7 to 2.4 m long and weighing, on average, only 80 kg, is the smallest of the dolphins inhabiting Icelandic waters. Males are a bit larger than females.

The common dolphin has a rather slender, perfectly streamlined body, unlike the white-beaked and Atlantic white-sided dolphins, which are thicker, more powerfully built and somewhat larger. The common dolphin's snout is rather long and narrow, clearly demarcated from a relatively high forehead. Its dorsal fin, sharp and curved slightly backward, is situated in the centre of the back, and the flippers and flukes are rather small. It has 80 to 110 teeth in its upper and lower jaws.

The upper part of the dolphin, its snout and flippers are black for the most part or dark-grey, but farthest forward, its sides are yellowish or pale green, becoming light-grey farther back. On the underbelly, the colouring is white. The geographical variations of this species being very many, the colour pattern, which is in fact very complex, can vary greatly, depending on in precisely what part of the world this dolphin species is found.

The common dolphin is believed to be the most numerous of dolphin species in the ocean and even of all mammals on earth, at least the bigger ones. However, the actual size of the stock is totally unknown, although it has been estimated that in the North Pacific alone, where the most research on the common dolphin has been done, there are at least 1,000,000 animals. Based on this information, there could well be two, three or even more millions of common dolphins because they are found in all the oceans. They inhabit waters close to land and in the inland seas like the Mediterranean, the Black Sea, the Red Sea and the Persian Gulf, as well as on the high seas. The only exception is in the coldest waters around both poles. There is also some documentation of the common dolphin going into fresh water, for example, up the Hudson River in New York in the United States. At least two specimens have been found dead along its banks. One was 135 km inland and the other 270 km from the ocean. These dolphins generally travel in groups of 10 to 500, although there are, in fact, many instances of schools of thousands of animals. They swim fast and can reach great speeds, up to 64 km per hour. They can often be seen following ships and even whales, such as fin whales, Gray whales, humpbacks and blue whales. Individual freedom is believed to be more prevalent among common dolphins than among other dolphins. However, they co-operate at a fairly high level in hunting for food. They hunt mostly small schooling fish like herring, anchovies and sardines, as well as squid and octopus. Usually, they hunt for food at a depth of about 40 m, although one common dolphin was observed diving to 280 m in pursuit of food, staying underwater for a full eight minutes.

It is not known whether the common dolphin is migratory.

Toothed whales employ a kind of sonar technology, in addition to sight and hearing, for their hunting. Some can even cripple their prey with bursts of high-frequency sound.

Researchers, however, have observed a definite transfer of animals from one area to another according to season. However, they have no basis to conclude anything about the nature of the transfer. At least, nothing is known of the migratory routes. Scientists also disagree on how to interpret the many, dissimilar colour variations of this dolphin and the size differences as well, depending on where in the world the animal is found.

Some wish to classify them under several different sub-species, or even have more than one species, whereas others choose to move more slowly. This debate is unlikely to be resolved soon since the matter, to put it mildly, is complicated. However, it is clear that short-nosed animals are involved on the one hand, and long-nosed animals on the other.

Very little is known about mating and birth, except in a very small area in the eastern part of the North Pacific. Pregnancy there seems to take 10 to 11 months, with calves being born in the spring, summer or autumn. They nurse for 14 to 19 months. The females mature sexually when 6 to 7 years old, while males do so at 5 to 12 years of age. Various things indicate that nursing females and those about to give birth keep away from the main group. Otherwise, little is known about the main group's composition. However, given the geographic variations of this dolphin mentioned above, it could well be that calves are born in equatorial waters all year round, but at only certain times of the year in colder regions.

The common dolphin rarely strands on beaches and dies. Undoubtedly this is due, in part, to its more common habitation in the open ocean than near land. When stranding does happen, though, generally only one or a few animals are involved at a time. The occurrences can often be traced to diseases infesting the animals, for example, parasitic worms in the head and ear canals that have damaged or confused the animal's high-frequency apparatus. Only one certain instance of a common dolphin running aground in Iceland is known.

bottlenose dolphin
Tursiops truncatus

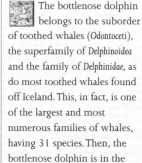 The bottlenose dolphin belongs to the suborder of toothed whales (*Odontoceti*), the superfamily of *Delphinoidea* and the family of *Delphinidae*, as do most toothed whales found off Iceland. This, in fact, is one of the largest and most numerous families of whales, having 31 species. Then, the bottlenose dolphin is in the subfamily *Delphininae* and finally in the genus *Tursiops*, of which it is the sole member.

The bottlenose dolphin has a very rakish build, or what one might call curvaceous, and is about 1.9 to 3.9 m long. The difference in length is determined by the stock and variant of the species to which the animal belongs. There are at least three subspecies. One is in the Atlantic Ocean and its contiguous inland seas. This subspecies is saliently the largest. Then, there are two subspecies in the Pacific Ocean and its contiguous inland seas, to both the North and South. Furthermore, males are a little bigger than females. The animal's coloration also varies by subspecies. Usually, however, it is mostly dark-grey on its back, light-grey on the sides and either pink or white underneath. Older animals often have blotches on the underbelly. The subspecies in the North Pacific are often brown on top, rather than grey.

The dolphin's snout is short and of variable thickness. The lower jaw is longer than the upper one. The dorsal fin, in the middle of the back, curves backward, as is typical of the smaller species of dolphin. The flippers are rather small. Besides being divided into the previously mentioned subspecies (*T.*

t. truncatus (in the Atlantic O-cean), T. t. gilli (in the Pacific Ocean) and T. t. aduncus (in the Red Sea and the Indian O-cean)), there are also two eco-logical variations of the bottle-nose dolphin. On the one hand, there are the animals inhabiting shallows that keep close to the coast where the depth is less than 20 m. On the other hand, there are animals of the high seas.

The bottlenose dolphin has 18 to 26 pairs of teeth in each jaw, that is, 72 to 104 teeth altogether. Its main diet is any kind of fish, especially school-ing groundfish, and also squid and octopus, etc. The animals co-operate when hunting for food. The feeding habits of shallow-water and deep-water animals vary, as might be ex-pected.

The bottlenose dolphin lives in oceans all over the world and is believed to be very common in them all. In other respects,

Many recognise the star of television and cinema, Flipper, which was (and is) a bottlenose dolphin.

the size of the stock is not known. The bottlenose dolphin, for example, is found along the entire East Coast of the United States, off Florida and in the Gulf of Mexico. People in the US regard this as the one and only true dolphin. It often enters harbours and coastal resort are-

as, playfully following boats that pass by.

This is the species of dolphin most often seen in aquariums, movies and on television. It can perform all kinds of feats and tricks. It is also the species most thoroughly researched by scientists.

The bottlenose dolphin commonly travels in groups of 10 to 40 animals, but has also been known to form groups of many dozens or even hundreds of animals. Generally, the shallow-water groups have fewer members than the deep-water groups.

Icelandic folklore held the bottlenose dolphin to be a horribly dangerous whale, said to attack every boat to destroy it. Fishermen today are not familiar with the bottlenose dolphin behaving in this way, and it may be that this descrip-tion pertains to another species. Another explanation is possible: that a bottlenose dolphin

happened once, accidentally, to destroy a boat on Icelandic fish-ing grounds. That is, the animal miscalculated a leap, landing on the boat, with serious conse-quences for the occupants, and thus the story got started.

Bottlenose dolphins often accompany long-finned pilot whales. Experts believe that the whales are chasing squid and octopus. The deep-water bottlenose dolphin is thought capable of diving to a depth of 600 m for food.

The animals generally mate in the spring and summer, with calves being born 12 to 13 months later. The calf nurses for approximately 18 months, although it starts to eat fish at 6 months of age. The females mature sexually at the age of 9 or 10 and bear young every 2 to 3 years. The males, however, do not mature sexually until they are 10 to 13 years old. Some hunting of the bottlenose dolphin has been done through

the ages, especially in the West Indies, off West Africa and in the Indian Ocean and Japan. The Soviets also hunted them in the Black Sea until 1960, and, to some degree, the Turks. This was stopped, for the most part, in the last several decades.

Rapidly rising pollution levels are one of the chief threats today to many species of whale, including the bottlenose dolphin.

striped dolphin
Stenella coeruleoalba

The striped dolphin belongs to the suborder of toothed whales (Odontoceti), the superfamily of Delphinoidea, the family of Delphinidae, which is the most diverse whale family, with 31 species altogether. Then, it is in the subfamily Delphininae and, finally, in the genus Stenella.

Males are slightly larger than females. The animal's build is extremely slender and supple, most resembling that of the common dolphin.

The snout is long and thin. The striped dolphin has 90 to 100 conical, sharp-pointed teeth. Its dorsal fin stands rather high and sweeps backward at the narrowing top. The flukes are relatively small. The tail stock is also rather narrow, and, in fact, insubstantial in appearance for a dolphin.

The animal's coloration can vary greatly, although it is generally dark-grey or brown on top, or even bluish. The same holds for the snout and flippers. The sides, however, are light-grey and the underbelly white. All these colours blend into a very complex, long-striped pattern.

The striped dolphin has a sportive nature and is very gregarious, as is common among dolphins. It often follows ships and boats, often hurtling along and leaping or doing aerobatics. Most often, several hundred animals are seen together, but shoals can also number in the thousands.

The internal organisation of these groups is not known except in certain areas, for example, off Japan. There, there seems to be a three-group division: first, very young, sexually immature animals; second, unmated males and females; and third, mated whales. After a certain time has passed, calves move into the young-animal groups, where they stay for a few years until they join the unmated groups and so forth from there. These movements are constant.

The distribution area of the striped dolphin covers all the oceans of the world, except the very coldest. The animals seem to keep more to the deep sea than to coastlines.

The striped dolphin's main diet is any sort of small pelagic fish, squid and octopus (less than 30 cm long) and shrimp. The stomach contents of one dolphin caught off South Africa were examined. The remains of 14 species of small fish and five species of squid and octopus were found.

The animals in the western part of the North Pacific, where most of the research on this dolphin has been done, seem to mature sexually at 5 to 9 years of age. Mating is believed to occur in the spring and summer. Pregnancy lasts about 12 months. After three months, the new-born calves begin to feed on things other than their mother's milk, but they continue in the mother's care for another 15 months.

The striped dolphin is in all likelihood migratory, although its seasonal routes are not known precisely, except in certain areas, for example, off Japan. These animals travel south to the East China Sea when winter approaches and return in the spring.

These dolphins sometimes swim up on beaches and die, either singly or a few together. However, no large groups are known to have done this. For many centuries, Japanese fishermen have hunted striped dolphins for food, at first with hand-held harpoons or by driving the animals onto land. Later, they employed more modern methods. From 1950 to 1960, modern fishing, on average, resulted in 15,000 animals being caught annually. Today, these figures have decreased greatly, being 2,000 to 4,000. In other areas like Papua New Guinea and the Solomon Islands, some animals are taken, but with primitive methods. Also, tuna fishers' Danish seine in the Eastern Pacific has killed many striped dolphins through the years. Little is known about other natural enemies, although sharks as well as killer whales are probably among them.

A striped dolphin has only once washed up on the shores of Iceland. This was in Öræfa-fjörur in 1984. It is not clear how this find should be interpreted. Perhaps this was an isolated phenomenon, that is, a wandering waif. Or, and this is not at all out of the question, the species is sometimes off Iceland, especially off the south and south-eastern coasts. It should be recalled that it is difficult to distinguish between dolphin species in the open ocean since they commonly swim fast and, in addition, resemble each other. Nor does it help that the weather conditions are very seldom ideal, that is, calm and bright. Without doubt, this question will be cleared up in the future with more research by cetologists and the vigilance of fishermen and beachcombers, on the look-out for whatever the sea has washed ashore.

Despite its playfulness, the striped dolphin has not worked out for use in aquariums for some reason.

killer whale
Orcinus orca

The killer whale belongs to the suborder of toothed whales (Odontoceti), the dolphin superfamily (Delphinoidea) and the the most numerous family of whales, Delphinidae, having 31 species. The killer whale is in the subfamily of Orcinus, of which it is the only extant species.

Foreign references state that the fully grown male killer whales are, on average, about 7 m long and weigh 4.5 tons, while females are somewhat smaller, a bit over 6 m, weighing 3 tons. The size figures in Icelandic references are a bit higher, differing by a metre, putting males at 8 m, on average, and females at 7 m. In addition, there are instances of bigger males being found than are mentioned above. They were up to 9.5 m or more and weighed some 8 tons, and females of up to 8.5 m have been found, weighing about 7.5 tons.

The killer whale's coloration is very peculiarly mottled, although the colour separation is very clear and sharp. The upper part of the whale is mostly dark, but the white patches lying behind both eyes evoke the above-mentioned colour pattern. In the same fashion, there is a greyish patch or spot behind the dorsal fin. The underbelly, on the other hand, is snow-white, the colour reaching somewhat up on the body behind the mid-section in a distinctive wing-shape.

The proboscis is rounded and broad, lacking the typical dolphin nose lines, but nevertheless showing an incipient nose bulge; the flippers, shaped like paddles, are rather large; and the dorsal fin is tall and straight, especially on older males, where it can be approximately 2 m high. Proportionally,

The male Keiko, which was caught off the coast of Iceland, and later played the title role in the films, Free Willy I and II, is probably the best known killer whale today. Ideas about returning him to his natural environment off Iceland are now being discussed.

this is the biggest dorsal fin of any whale. The females generally have a more moderate dorsal fin, although still big.

The killer whales of the North and South Poles differ somewhat in appearance, especially regarding the dark coloration on the upper body. On the whales in the Northern Hemisphere, the colour is coal black, while the killer whale of the Southern Hemisphere is dark-grey. Some specialists also believe that the white patches behind the eyes can also be changeable or variously large, depending on whether the animal is from the North or the South.

The killer whale has 40 to 56 elliptical teeth in its jaw that are up to 10 cm long. It does not section its prey in parts and chew it, but uses these teeth only to catch and kill. It then swallows the prey in one gulp, unless it is extremely large.

To say the least, the killer whale lives on very diverse diet. Written references exist for at least 24 different species of whale, five species of animals with flippers (that is, seals and the like), 30 species of fish, seven species of bird and two kinds of squid and octopus, in addition to many other animals.

Off Iceland, the killer whale eats mainly herring, capelin, squid and octopus, but also takes seals, walruses and whales. In other oceans, penguins can be added to this, where found, and various large fish, such as shark and skate. It has even been attested that the remains of a polar bear were found in a killer whale's stomach. Experts think that the killer whale needs to eat the equivalent of up to 5% of its weight every day. For a male weighing 5 tons, that makes 250 kg.

In hunting herring, the killer whale sometimes employs the method of swimming around the shoals to consolidate them, finally swiping the fish with its flukes to kill them. It then eats its kill leisurely. There are stories in many parts of the world, both ancient and contemporary, about the daring and organised hunting methods of killer whales when it comes to

Collections of Icelandic folktales are filled with descriptions of "evil whales" that attack fishermen out on the ocean, trying to destroy them. And sometimes succeeded. Also, annals and other sources occasionally say the same things. It would be too easy to reject them as absurdities and nonsense because clearly something happened to spark these accounts.

*Killer whales have many teeth, swim fast and forcibly and are daring. They often take seals and even attack large whales. Both old and new examples of this abound. The King's Mirror from the 13th century, for example, says: "They have as many teeth as dogs and resemble attacking the giants of the sea, such as the bowhead whale (*Balaena mysticetus*), humpback whale (*Megaptera novaeangliae*) and blue whale (*Balaenoptera musculus*).*

them in rapacity toward other whales as dogs toward other animals because they gather in large groups and descend upon large whales, and where a great whale is alone, they bite it and worry it until it dies…" Despite accounts like this one, there are no known instances of killer whales, in their own environment, having attacked people simply to kill and eat them. In 1911, when the Peter Scott expedition was preparing a final attempt to reach the South Pole, eight killer whales tried to reach the sled dogs that had been tied to an ice arch. One expedition member, photographer Herbert Pointing, was present. The killer whales failed to nab their prey and disappeared. The story started circulating (illustrated, cf. above), but the dogs, the focus of the action, were forgotten. This seemed to be proof that killer whales were bloodthirsty animals, to be watched out for and avoided. The truth did not emerge until 1960 when scientists started to research killer whales in earnest.

Greenlandic fishermen truly fear killer

The killer whale is very gregarious, as is, in fact, common among dolphins, often travelling in groups of 3-25 animals, or even larger. The most common

whales, paddling their canoes to land or quickly into hiding when killer whales approach because, on one occasion, they attacked a boat. However, as in the previous instance, the animals' behaviour can be easily explained. The fishermen, in fact, were towing a dead seal. Other accounts, for example, when people shooting a movie swam among killer whales that were hunting seals off the Patagonian coast of Argentina, confirm that they have no interest in sinking their teeth into Homo sapiens. The fact that these animals are predators is another matter. They must never be underestimated under any circumstances. This would be foolish because, as with humans, there could always be exceptions to the rule. A deviant individual could be involved or, simply, a very hungry one. One need hardly ask about the outcome of such an encounter.

configuration is one fully grown male and several mates of his, in addition to their calves, younger and older. Other males gather in bachelor groups.

The killer whale swims, on average, 10-15 km per hour on long journeys, although it can go up to 50 km per hour, if required. It is, by far, the largest and fastest member of its family. This whale is found in all oceans of the world, in shallow waters as well as on the high seas. It feels most at home at shallow depths, but can also dive deep, up to 1,000 m if it cares to do so. Such a dive takes only 20 minutes because of the animal's natural speed and power. Regular migratory routes for the killer whale are difficult to identify. However, they do move somewhat according to the seasons. Most experts believe they change location randomly in pursuit of the best hunting. Off Iceland, for example, they certainly follow herring and capelin migrations and are therefore commonly seen off Iceland's coasts, especially in the summer and autumn. In fact, it is thought that there are few, if any, places in the world where this species of whale is more abundant than in Iceland, and then in certain areas of the Pacific Ocean and at the South Pole.

Female killer whales mature sexually at age 8 to 10 years, but males not until they are about 16 years old. Mating and pregnancy seem to occur at all times of the year. A pregnancy lasts 12 to 16 months. The calf, when born, is about 2.1 to 2.5 m long and weighs 180 kg.

For a long time, fishermen have borne a grudge against killer whales, especially because of the suspicion and, actually, accusations that they rob and ruin their nets. The fishermen, more often than not, have tried to take some measures against this.

In Canada, fishermen had a similar problem, and the country's Government decided to fund experiments with killer-prow attachments to ships, like those on ancient Greek boats, to ram the whales. No accounts of the results are available.

Through the centuries, some nations have utilised the killer whale for food, although generally there has not been any organised hunting of the animal, as there has been for great whales. American whalers in the 18th and 19th centuries did, on occasion, kill these animals when the prey that they were actually hunting was not seen. However, this was never done on a large scale. Between 1938 and 1981, on the other hand, the Norwegians took some 2,400 killer whales in the North-east Atlantic and 50 more off the southern tip of Greenland, and the Japanese caught about 1,200 animals in the ocean off their own shores in the years 1953 to 1977. The Soviets killed 270 animals in the North-west Pacific in the period 1953 to 1964.

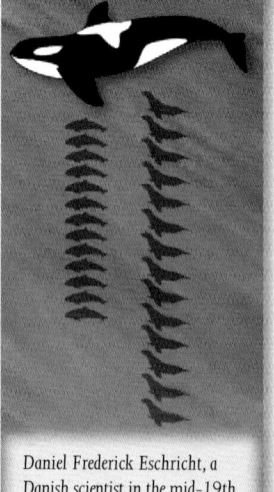

Daniel Frederick Eschricht, a Danish scientist in the mid-19th century, reported the stomach contents of a killer whale about 5 m long that had stranded and died. The stomach held 13 porpoises and 14 seals, and a fifteenth seal, which was stuck in the animal's gullet, was probably what killed it.

In the Southern Hemisphere, up until 1953, the killer whale was left alone. Then, the Soviets

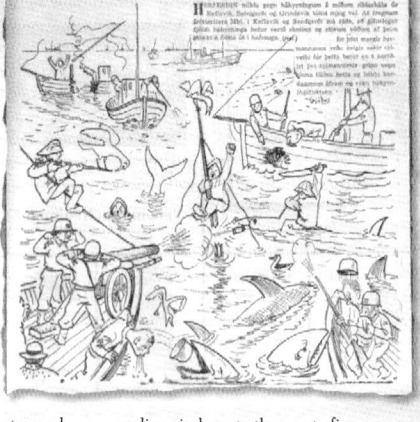

Around the middle of this century and later, it was quite common for the Icelandic Government to request the military at the NATO base in Keflavík for assistance in scaring off killer whales that disturbed fishing on the herring banks. At first, the military was sent with their boats to the grounds, and they shot the animals with rifles. But sometimes this was not enough. When the killer whales were once very aggressive toward herring nets off the Reykjanes Peninsula (SW Iceland), the Iceland Defence Force reacted harshly, sending airplanes to the area to fire machine guns at the schools and drop depth charges. Estimates are that many hundred animals were killed. This picture appeared in 1954 issue of The Mirror.

started hunting them there, killing 1,700 animals between then and 1980.

In recent years, a great interest has sprung up to get killer whales for aquariums all over the world. For this purpose, from 1962 to 1973, 67 killer whales were captured alive off North America in the Pacific Ocean, that is, off British Columbia and Washington State. In Iceland, Jón Kr. Gunnarsson, then Director of the Aquarium in Hafnarfjordur, pioneered in this enterprise in the autumn of 1975. He then sailed the fishing ship, Gudrún GK 27, in search of killer whales and has done so many times since then.

Over the period 1975 to 1988, 84 killer whales were captured in this way. Animals from Iceland have been exported very widely, especially to the countries of Europe, but also to the United States, Argentina, Brazil, Mexico, Japan and Hong Kong. Currently, there are, to put it mildly, conflicting views on the propriety of such hunting, with the strongest voice against this coming from Greenpeace adherents.

long-finned pilot whale
Globicephala melas

 The long-finned pilot whale belongs to the suborder of toothed whales (*Odontoceti*), the superfamily of *Delphinoidea* and the family of *Delphinidae*. Altogether, this family has 31 species and is the most numerous of all whale families. The long-finned pilot whale also belongs to the subfamily of *Globicephalinae* and, finally, the genus *Globicephala*, which it shares with the short-finned pilot whale.

Fully-grown, male long-finned pilot whales are, on average, about 5.5 to 6 m long and weigh 3.5 tons. The females are a bit smaller or about 4 to 5 m and weigh about 1.8 tons. Some males larger than those mentioned above have been documented, or up to 8.5 m long, and females 6 m long.

Adult animals are mostly black in colour, except for a trace of grey behind the high and rounded dorsal fin, similar to that on the killer whale. In addition, a white or light-grey stripe on the underbelly stretches almost to the head where it divides to make an anchorshaped pattern. The upper half of younger animals is not as dark.

This whale's flippers are long and narrow and are regarded as one of its chief identifying characteristics. Also, its forehead is very high and bulbous, especially in older males. There are 8 to 13 pairs of teeth in each jaw.

The long-finned pilot whale is primarily a deep-sea whale, appearing to prefer waters of 0°-25°C. Nevertheless, it regularly comes into shallow waters at certain times of the year, looking for food, as experts believe.

There are two subspecies of long-finned pilot whale. The home waters of one of them, *G. m. melas*, is the North Atlantic, from south-west Greenland, Iceland and the Barents Sea in the North to Cape Hatteras in North America and the north-west coast of Africa in the South. The Gulf of St. Lawrence, the Baltic and Mediterranean Seas are included in these locations. The other subspecies, *G. m. edwardi*, is common in the whole Southern Hemisphere, in the Atlantic, Pacific and Indian Oceans.

The long-finned pilot whale is a polygamous animal.

The females mature sexually at about six years of age and give birth every three years. The term of pregnancy is estimated to be 16 months. Calves are usually born in August. They suckle for 20 months or so. The males do not mature sexually until 12 to 20 years of age, having then attained a length of 5 m.

Long-finned pilot whales are very sociable, generally travelling in large groups of several hundred animals. One source even documents a school of 3,000 animals. The commonest size of long-finned pilot whale schools, however, is 15 to 200. Very often, they are seen in the company of other dolphins, for example, the common dolphin (*Delphinus delphis*) and the bottlenose dolphin (*Tursiops truncatus*).

Another characteristic of these animals is that they sleep very tightly grouped, half-scraping beneath the surface, their flippers touching.

Approaching long-finned pilot whales at sea is easy; nevertheless, they are not eager to approach ships or follow them. This is unlike the predisposition of most other species of dolphin. The long-finned pilot whale seldom dives for longer than 5 to 10 minutes at a time and searches for food at a depth of 30 to 60 m on average. It can, nevertheless, dive to a depth of 600 m or more if need be. But since hunting long-finned pilot whales is nowhere regarded as an industry, people have little interest in researching this species, and relatively little is therefore known about its habits.

Nevertheless, it is known that the long-finned pilot whale is commonly all around Iceland in the summer and comes up to the north-west and west coast in the autumn (August, September and October), hunting its favourite food, squid (*Todarodes sagittatus*). Off the north-east, east and south-east coast, the whale is not as common. In addition to the food mentioned above, the whale also feeds on various species of schooling fish.

Quite often, the long-finned pilot whale will beach itself, that is, it will swim up on the beach and get stranded. This, in fact, also occurs with other

The picture shows long-finned pilot whales stranded near Thorlákshöfn in October 1986. People generally disagree on why this happens. The hypotheses vary. For example, one is that certain magnetic spots in Iceland scramble the animals' high-frequency systems. Another is that the leader whale gets sick, perhaps from parasites in its ears, causing a breakdown of its navigational system so that it cannot avoid what lies in front of it. Regarding the long-finned pilot whale specifically, the reason for the frequent strandings may be that it is strictly a whale of the open ocean that approaches land only at certains times of the year. These times obviously put the whale at greater than normal risk since the open ocean holds no shallows to guard against.

species of whale, although not nearly as often. People generally disagree on the reason for this beaching behaviour, and there are various hypotheses. For example, one is that there are certain magnetic patches on land that confuse the animals' high-frequency system. Another hypothesis is that the leader whale gets sick, perhaps because of parasites in its ears, so that its navigation system breaks down and it cannot detect what

lies ahead. Another reason for these frequent incidents may be traced to the long-finned pilot whale's being mainly a deep-sea creature that comes up to land only at certain times of the year, where it is conceivably more at risk than otherwise. For centuries, the Faeroese have utilised the long-finned pilot whale as food, and probably, their utilisation has been the greatest of any country. Their written history of such fisheries goes all the way back to 1584.

The first 300 years, or until 1884, they caught 120,000 animals off the islands, which is approximately 400 each year.

Over the 42-year period from 1936 to 1978, they took, on average, 1,552 animals per year. Today, the annual take is very similar, or about 1,500 animals per year.

Other countries have not caught as many animals, but have taken a considerable quantity over the years. The

Faeroe Islands excepted, this species has been hunted chiefly in the Orkneys, the Shetland Islands, Norway, Greenland and, not least, Newfoundland.

In earlier times, Icelanders considered a beached long-finned pilot whale a great asset for the household. People would often try to promote this occurrence directly, as the Faeroese did. Many Icelandic sources cite such instances. In 1705, for example, 40 long-finned pilot whales were driven onto the beach at Innri-Njardvík and killed, and in 1815, 150 long-finned pilot whales were driven onto land there. In September of 1823, many animals were driven into Hlídarhúsabót, Reykjavík Harbour. In 1878, many animals were driven into Stakksfjordur and killed on the Njardvík shore. However, one of the biggest long-finned pilot whale killings in recent times was in 1929 when 1,000 animals ran up on the beach in

Ófeigsfjordur on Strandir. Most of the animals, however, escaped with the next high tide. In 1934, 50 long-finned pilot whales ran ashore in the Reykjavík area, in Fossvogur. In 1939, whales were driven ashore in Njardvík. About 40 animals ran ashore in Gufunes in 1945 where the Reykjavík municipal garbage dump was later situated. Whales again ran aground in Njardvík in 1957. In 1984, 30 long-finned pilot whales came up on the beach at Rif on the Snæfellsnes Peninsula, and in 1986, two years later, upwards of 200 animals became stranded at night in Thorlákshöfn.

northern bottlenose whale
Hyperoodon ampullatus

 The northern bottlenose whale belongs to the suborder of toothed whales (*Odontoceti*), the superfamily of beaked whales (*Ziphioidea*) and the family of Ziphiidae. It is third largest in this group, with only Beard's beaked whale (*Berardius bairdii*) and Arnaud's beaked whale (*Berardius arnuxii*) being larger. Finally, the northern bottlenose whale is of the genus *Hyperoodon*.

The northern bottlenose whale can grow to over 9 m, the Beard's beaked whale to 10 m and the Arnaud's beaked whale up to 13 m. Fully grown males off Iceland are, on average, 8.4 m long, while females average 7.2 m.

In many ways, the northern bottlenose whale is rather unlike its near relatives in both appearance and nature. It is, in fact, the only whale in this family about which anything is really known. Its nose is narrow and the forehead high and bulbous, especially in older males. The shape of the nose, which resembles a bottleneck, is the source of the whale's name, "bottlenose".

At the front of the animal's lower jaw on both sides, there are two teeth, 2-4 cm long. However, they do not erupt from the gums except in male animals in their 15th to 17th year. All females are, therefore, without teeth to all appearances.

The northern bottlenose whale's colouring can vary greatly, but most commonly the whale is grey-black or dark brown on its upper half and somewhat lighter on its underside. With increasing age, some of the animals take on a very light colouring all over, with some of them becoming almost

A northern bottlenose whale readies its flukes for lob-tailing. Picture by Fridtjof Nansen.

white on their forehead and nose.

The eyes sit right behind and above the corners of the mouth. The flippers, which are very small, are a little in back of the head. The back fin, about 30 cm high, is relatively far back. The flukes, as is the case in other beaked whales, are not notched in the middle.

The northern bottlenose whale is most at home in the deep sea, commonly staying in the open ocean beyond continental shelf boundaries, where the depth is 1,000 m or more.

Unlike other beaked whales that are mysterious and seldom seen, the northern bottlenose whale is very sociable, willingly approaching ships and boats. It is also known for its unique faithfulness and devotion to its own species. The whale does not desert a wounded companion while it is still alive.

Formerly, whalers took unmerciful advantage of this trait. In fact, this trait of support in times of need pertains to many other whale species as well. The northern bottlenose whale is, for the most part, a migratory whale, as are most other toothed whales. They are found in the North Atlantic and Arctic Oceans, although seeing them in the north-western Atlantic is rather rare. During the summer, you can find this whale all around Iceland, but it is most commonly found in the ocean between Iceland and Jan Mayen. They range as far as the edge of the Arctic ice cap and even go a few kilometres in under it. The adult males are thought to go farther north than any other members of the species. As autumn approaches, though, the northern bottlenose whale moves south. Its winter areas are, for the most part, in the ocean areas between New York and the Mediterranean, but these whales can range as far south as the Cape Verde Islands off the West Coast of Africa. It may, however, be that a certain portion or isolated stocks do not go as far south as others, but stay in the ocean between Iceland, Norway and the Faeroe Islands.

In the Southern Hemisphere, another bottlenose whale species can be found that is a bit smaller than the species in the North. It is called the southern bottlenose whale (*Hyperoodon planifrons*). Little is known about it.

Bottlenose whales are usually solitary, or there are a few of them together. Young females prefer to be in small groups of 5-10 animals with their calves. Sometimes, however, larger and more mixed groups can be seen.

The northern bottlenose whale, like other beaked whales, is a very deep diver, perhaps going the deepest of any whale. At least, some scientists believe that this whale dives farther than all other whales, going farther down than even the sperm whale that has long been regarded as the uncrowned king in this respect. Here, no claims will be made about this, but it is a fact that northern bottlenose whales were once observed on a dive lasting 120 minutes. The sperm whale is known to dive for a similar length of time. The circumstances, however, were a bit special in this instance: the animals, harpoons deep in them, were fleeing from whalers. There is therefore little reason to suppose that this was a typical dive. Furthermore, when the northern bottlenose whales finally broke, they hardly blew at all.

The northern bottlenose whale feeds almost entirely on squid and octopus. In the ocean off Norway, it mainly eats giant squid (*Gonatus fabricii*), but off Iceland, it also feeds on squid (*Todarodes sagittatus*) and sometimes herring, shrimp and star fish.

The northern bottlenose whale matures sexually at the age of 9 to 12 years. The mating season is in the spring and early summer. Pregnancy lasts about 12 months with calves being born in April or May. Females are believed to bear offspring every other year.

Organised whaling of the northern bottlenose whale began in the latter half of the 19th century, with many being taken in the seas north of Iceland. Scottish whalers from Dundee led the way, followed by the Norwegians. From 1882 to 1920, some 50,000 animals were taken. The biggest year was 1896 with 2,864 whales. Six thousand more were caught from 1927 to 1973. Demand was especially great for the northern bottlenose whale's oil that is in its head, not dissimilar to that of the sperm whale, although in liquid form. It is one of the fattiest substances known in nature, and it was used as a laxative, oil and salve. The meat was also processed and used as fodder for animals. In 1977 the northern bottlenose whale became a protected species and remains so today. The size of the stock is not known. It should, however, be mentioned that the Marine Research Institute of Iceland, in co-operation with Denmark, the Faeroe Islands, Norway and Spain, sponsored a whale survey

The Active from Dundee in Scotland. This was one of the ships that pursued whales in the oceans of the North in the latter part of the 19th century.

in a limited area of the North Atlantic in the summer of 1987. A considerable number of northern bottlenose whales were found off the continental shelf west of Iceland and also in the deeps off the Eastern Fjords. Altogether, the surveyors saw 6,000 animals, a quantity believed to be only 30% of the whole population of these areas. Northern bottlenose whales, like sperm whales, are difficult to count with precision because, as mentioned above, they are very prodigious divers. Just finding them on the surface is therefore a matter of chance. The quantity, 15,000 to 20,000 animals, if correctly estimated, came as a bit of a surprise.

cuvier's beaked whale
ZIPHIUS CAVIROSTRIS

Cuvier's beaked whale belongs to the suborder of toothed whales (Odontoceti), the superfamily of beaked whales (Ziphioidea) and the family of Ziphiidae, which is one branch of toothed whales with 20 species, so far as known. Finally, Cuvier's beaked whale is in the genus of Ziphius.

These are all average-sized whales, 3-13 m long, which are found in all oceans. Nevertheless, little is known about most of them.

They are prodigious swimmers and can dive very deep. Some experts even believe they can surpass the sperm whale in this respect, at least regarding the length of diving time and perhaps depth, also.

Females of the species are believed to be a bit bigger than males, which is the exception among toothed whales.

The Cuvier's beaked whale is somewhat corpulent and cylindrical, with a medium-sized head, ending in a short, broad nose. Its forehead is not very high, unlike other beaked whales. The flippers are rather small as are the dorsal fin and flukes. Also, its lower jaw is considerably longer than the upper jaw.

It has only two teeth, about 8 cm long, at the very front of the lower jaw; they generally erupt only in male animals. The Cuvier's beaked whale is, for the most part, a deep-sea whale, and is believed to be found in all the oceans in the world, except for the coldest locales, that is, the Arctic and Antarctic Oceans. If they have migratory routes, nothing is known of them   People most commonly sight single animals, travelling alone, and generally these are fully grown males. Or, they are sometimes seen in small groups of 2 to 7 animals. Otherwise, their internal division is not known. Larger groups of 15 or so animals have also been seen.

Cuvier's beaked whales have been seen to breach high and land clumsily. Likewise, people have noted a diving pattern similar to that of the humpback whale. That is, the whale starts its dive by lifting its flukes high into the air. Otherwise, what is known of Cuvier's beaked whales comes from beached individuals. This species, of all the beaked whales, is the one most frequently washed ashore dead. The size of the stock is, however, completely unknown, but its distribution, which is one of the widest of any whale stock – that is, all over the earth's oceans, except for the coldest – undeniably indicates something about the stock size.

The coloration of Cuvier's beaked whales is diverse, being determined by sex, age and area. In the Pacific Ocean, its main colour is generally a light brown, while it is light-grey or bluish in the Atlantic. The head is whitish-yellow, lightening with age, which is also true for the part of the back closest to the head. White blotches are on the underbelly. In addition, fully grown animals, especially males, have abrasions all over from strife amongst themselves or with other creatures of the ocean deeps.

Almost no references contain information on the length of pregnancy and giving birth. However, the calves are believed to be over 2.5 m when born. Experts think sexual maturity is attained when the animals reach a length of 5 m.

On average, the Cuvier's beaked whales dive for about 40 minutes at a time when hunting. Only the Japanese have, through the years, tried to hunt the Cuvier's beaked whale. Certainly the catch figures are not high. From 1965 to 1970, for example, only 13 to 60 animals per year were killed.

Cuvier's beaked whales have only been found twice off Iceland, in 1979 and 1981. In both instances, they were dead, beached on the coast off Öræfasveit. What this, in fact, means is difficult to say. As previously mentioned, this whale most commonly keeps to the deep-sea areas and is also very shy. Its blow is also small and indistinct, so some quantity could just as well be all around the country, at least off the south and south-eastern shores, although people have not seen it very often there.

blainville's beaked whale
Mesoplodon densirostris

Blainville's beaked whale belongs to the suborder of toothed whales (Odontoceti), the superfamily of beaked whales (Ziphioidea), the familiy of Ziphiidae and, finally, the genus Mesoplodon.

Whales of this genus have a very peculiar appearance, especially regarding the lower jaw of males. They generally have a well developed pair of teeth that stick out. These are commonly very slender and are like the tusks of a wild boar. Experts think that the whales use these giant teeth in fights with each other and also to kill the bigger squid and octopus that are the whale's main diet.

The jawbone of whales in this genus is heavy and dense, and, in the case of the Blainville's beaked whale, 34% denser than ivory. The size,

orientation and placement of the teeth vary by species. In Sowerby's beaked whale (Mesoplodon bidens), they are, for example, rather small, about 10 cm, and in the middle of the jaw. In the strap-toothed whale (Mesoplodon layardii), the teeth are very tall and curve backward, while in True's beaked whale, they are hardly visible and on the end of the snout.

To put it mildly, little is known of the ways of the 14 extant beaked whales of the world. Most of them (nine species) were not discovered until earlier this century, and one, for example, never had an official name until 1991 (Mesoplodon peruvianus, the smallest one). Other beaked whales are known only from a few beached specimens, and still others are not known to science except through a very few sightings in the open ocean.

The reason for this is undoubtedly that species of deep-sea whales are involved that generally keep strictly away from the continental shelf, therefore very seldom washing up on beaches. Experts therefore believe it likely that the high seas conceal more species of

In previous centuries, bones from whales were coveted by craftsmen. The pictures on this panel describe the crucifixion, burial and ascension of Jesus. It was carved by Bryjólfur Jónsson around 1600 and is now preserved in the National Museum of Iceland. The jawbones of beaked whales are the most famous in the animal kingdom, especially those of Blainville's beaked whale that are 34% denser than ivory. However, there are no accounts of Icelandic craftsmen utilising this material. A Blainville's beaked whale, in fact, has only been found once in Iceland, stranded and dead on the beach. This was the sixth such find in the world. On the other hand, ancient Icelandic lawbooks from the 12th century, as well as The King's Mirror (13th century), mention "swine whales", but exactly what species is meant is not clear. Bones from whales were also utilised for various other things. Women having difficulty delivering a baby, for example, were given whale-bone powder mixed with water or even wine. This was supposed to facilitate the birth.

beaked whales than are known today.

The little that can be said about Mesoplodon whales as a whole, in addition to what has already been mentioned, is that they are 3 to 7 m long; the flippers are 25 to 50 cm long; the dorsal fin is very small (15 cm high) and situated far back on the body; and the flukes are an estimated 1 m wide. The blowhole is in front, above the eyes. Also, the lower jaw is longer than the upper jaw.

A fully grown Blainville's beaked whale is black or dark-grey on its back and sides, but light-coloured on its snout and underbelly. In addition, the body is often covered with grey-white or pink, oblong and circular spots and scratches, especially on males.

The dorsal fin is very small, situated near the rear of the body, as is common in this whale family. The flippers are rather insubstantial and the flukes about 1 m wide, smooth on the back edge, that is, absolutely notchless.

Blainville's beaked whale, like other species in this family, is a deep-sea creature and said to be very withdrawn and shy. It is thought to be a great diver, going perhaps deeper than the sperm whale, which has long been regarded as the king of this sport. However, dives of 20 to 25 minutes are thought to be commonest. Its main diet is squid and octopus, small or large, and, perhaps, deep-sea fish as well, depending on what the whale can manage with the few teeth it has.

The whale's distribution is believed to cover the entire Atlantic and Pacific Oceans, excluding the coldest waters of the polar seas. However, Blainville's beaked whale, for whatever reason, has never been found or spotted off South America or the British Isles. The size of the stock is unknown, but its vast distribution nevertheless indicates that Blainville's beaked whale is, perhaps, the commonest *Mesoplodon* in the world, despite the failure of scientists to obtain more than about 20 animals so far. In the whale survey of 1989, expedition members remarked the number of *Mesoplodon* species seen far southwest of Iceland. But whether these were Blainville's beaked whale or Sowerby's beaked whale or some other species is not known.

Blainville's beaked whale often travels alone or in groups of a few (2 to 10). The composition of the groups is otherwise unknown.

Little is known about mating, pregnancy and birth, although experts believe calves mature sexually at the age of nine years. Blainville's beaked whale has been little hunted. The only thing known in this regard is that a few animals were once taken off Taiwan.

A Blainville's beaked whale was found on the beach of Vatnsleysuströnd in South-west Iceland in February 1910.

sowerby's beaked whale
Mesoplodon bidens

 Sowerby's beaked whale belongs to the suborder of toothed whales (*Odontoceti*), the superfamily of beaked whales (*Ziphioidea*) and the family of *Ziphiidae*. Then, it is in the genus *Mesoplodon*.

To put it mildly, little is known of the ways of the 14 extant beaked whales in the world, as mentioned earlier. Most of them (nine species) were not discovered until this century, and one species, for example, never had an official name until 1991 (*Mesoplodon peruvianus*, the smallest one). Other beaked whales are known only from a few stranded specimens, and still others are not known to science except through a very few sightings in the open ocean.

The reason for this is undoubtedly that species of deep-sea whales are involved that generally keep strictly away from the continental shelf, therefore very seldom washing up on beaches. Experts therefore believe it likely that the high seas conceal more species of beaked whales than are known today.

The little that can be said about *Mesoplodon* whales as a whole, in addition to what has already been mentioned, is that they are 3 to 7 m long. The flippers are 25 to 50 cm long, and the dorsal fin, which is very small (15 cm high), is situated far back on the body. The flukes are an estimated 1 m wide. The blowhole is in front, above the eyes. Also the lower jaw is longer than the upper jaw.

Sowerby's beaked whale is the species of this seldom-seen genus that most commonly washes up on beaches. In fact, it was the first of these whales to become known to science when in 1800 a dead male Sowerby's beaked whale was found washed ashore in Moray Fjord in North-eastern Scotland. This animal's skull is still in a museum at Oxford University in England. Later, the species were discovered one after the other.

Sowerby's beaked whale, compared with other whales of its genus, is medium-sized. It is about 4 to 5 m long, weighing up to 1.5 tons. Two tusks are in the middle of the male's jaw, but the females have no teeth. References disagree on this species' coloration, especially because most of the information comes from dead animals washed ashore. This condition is thought to darken the colours. Nevertheless, experts think that fully grown individuals are generally dark-grey on the back, perhaps even bluish, but a bit lighter underneath and with whitish spots covering the body.

Younger animals are believed to be lighter all over and with fewer spots.

The dead whales that are found, both of this species and of others in the genus, are often covered with scars. These probably result from intra-group struggles, being caused by the above-mentioned tusks.

Sowerby's beaked whale, as others of the same species, keeps to the high seas, travelling either alone or in small groups. Large shoals are rare.

Its main diet is squid and octopus, small and large. Experts believe that the animals hunt them at enormous depths. No figures, however, are given in this regard. In addition, the whale hunts small fish as much as possible.

Little is known of mating and birth.

Sowerby's beaked whale is thought to inhabit the northern part of the Atlantic Ocean, that is, the areas from Newfoundland to France and up to Eastern Greenland and Svalbard. The whale is the northernmost member of its genus. Experts also believe that there are more Sowerby's beaked whales near Europe than North America because animals that have stranded or washed ashore have been seen more often in Europe, including Iceland, Denmark, Norway, Sweden, the Baltic Sea coast of Germany, Holland, Belgium, France, the British Isles and all the way down to Madeira. Thus, the centre of their distribution area seems to be the North Sea and the surrounding areas.

On the other hand, Sowerby's beaked whales have only washed ashore in North America in the State of Massachusetts, Newfoundland and Labrador.

Experts even think that two stocks could be involved, one that moves between the Bay of Biscay and the Norwegian Sea and another that frequents the area of ocean off North America between Newfoundland and New England. Nevertheless, some intercourse between the stocks is thought to occur.

Concerning the size of the stock, no figures are known. However, in a 1989 field survey, scientists remarked how common the Mesoplodon species were far south-west of Iceland. Whether these were Sowerby's beaked whales or Blainville's beaked whales or some other species is not known.

sperm whale
Physeter macrocephalus

The sperm whale belongs to the suborder of toothed whales (Odontoceti), the superfamily Physeteroidea and the family of Physeteridae. The sperm whale is the largest of all known, extant toothed whales. It further belongs to the subfamily Physeterinae and the genus Physeter.

The upper part of the animal is umber or dark grey. Its sides are lighter, and its underside is silver grey. The flippers and eyes are relatively small and the dorsal fin nearly non-existent. It has 30 teeth, each estimated to be 20 cm long, almost all in the long and narrow lower jaw. The sperm whale's brain, weighing about 10 kg, is the largest known in extant animals. This species holds other records as well. Many people believe that it is the deepest diving whale, especially the male.

People got early evidence of this fact when sperm whales got tangled in submarine telephone cables an estimated 1,100 m under the surface of the sea. The findings of recent research were, nevertheless, surprising: these animals could dive to twice this depth. And, as if this were not enough, specialists suspect that sperm whales go even deeper, all the way down to 3,200 m. Generally, though, the sperm whale is believed to hunt for food at 300 to 400 m, with each dive taking about 15 minutes. Nevertheless, it is known that the sperm whale is capable of dives lasting a good 120 minutes.

The sperm whale's head, which accounts for more than one-third of its total length, is very special because it contains a large volume of an extraordinary kind of fish oil. Researchers believe that the whale uses the oil to facilitate its deep diving by moving it to and fro in the body, depending on whether the whale is headed up or down, and also to equalise pressure and increase the absorption of oxygen. The sperm whale dives into the blackest depths for good reason: one of its main sources of food, especially in warmer seas, the giant

Sperm whales have got tangled in telephone cables, 1,100 m under the surface of the sea.

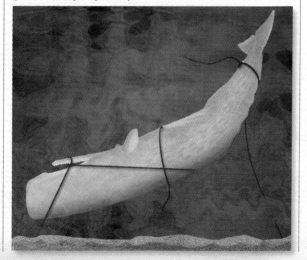

squid, is found there. In truth, one can often see circular scars on sperm whales from the cephalopods' suckers. Once these marks were measured to be of such diameter that their maker, by simple arithmetic, had to be at least 45 m long. In addition to this source of food for the sperm whale, there are various species of large fish, for example, tuna fish, giant skate, shark and also the giant octopus. Off Iceland, on the other hand, various species of smaller fish are the sperm whale's main food source, for example, lumpsucker, redfish, monkfish, cod, saithe and spotted catfish, but the whale also eats a considerable quantity of small octopus and squid.

The sperm whale, unlike other whales, takes many mates. Its social system, which is quite complex, is, in broad outline, based on herds, each of which includes individuals of a certain sex or age or other attribute. For example, a male travels with his harem, which usually consists of an estimated 20 to 30 adult animals. In the same way, young females group together, young males, etc.

Although the sperm whale is found all over the earth, it is above all a whale of warm seas.

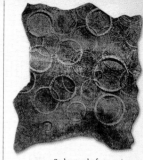

Sucker marks from a giant squid or octopus on a sperm whale's skin.

Sperm whale in the cold waters off Iceland are all adult males, either old individuals travelling alone after having lost their harem or young, inexperienced animals in groups of 10 to 20, awaiting their time. These are males aged 12 to 54. The winter grounds in the North Atlantic are near the Cape Verde and Canary Islands.

Mating is principally in April when the herds, which can each have up to 1,000 animals, are on their way north. Pregnancy lasts about 16 months, with calves being born in the summer. A new-born sperm whale nurses for 12 months. Specialists think that females bear young every three years. Sperm whale females mature sexually when they are 7 to 13 years old and have reached a length of 8 to 9 m. Males, however, do not mature until they are 18 to 21 years old and have reached a length of 11 to 12 m. Even then, they have to wait several more years before they can break into the ranks of harem holders.

In previous centuries, the sperm whale was common in seas all over the earth. However, terrible stories were told of the whale, and out of fear, it was left alone. Then in 1712, American whalers out of Nantucket in Massachusetts found a school of sperm whales. One of them frivolously harpooned one of the whales. Catching it went

The sperm whale's methods for gathering food are not entirely clear since the whale does this in the dark of the ocean deeps. There are, nevertheless, various ideas about this. One is that the whale settles on the bottom with its maw open, seizing all that wanders in. Another more likely one is that the whale swims along the bottom with its lower jaw dangling and sinks its teeth into whatever it encounters. A third idea is a mixture of the above methods. The sperm whale lies on or swims along the bottom. When it senses prey ahead, it emits sound waves to paralyse it and finally sucks it in somehow. The teeth do not seem to be essential, most of the time, anyway. However, they can come in handy because giant squid and octopus are a sperm whale's main diet, especially in warmer waters. These tentacled creatures grow to huge sizes. Sucker marks on a sperm whale's skin, 20 cm in diameter, were once measured. This indicates that the owner of the suckers was at least 45 m long.

well, and the profit proved to be great. From that moment, sperm whale fishing on a gargantuan scale was set in

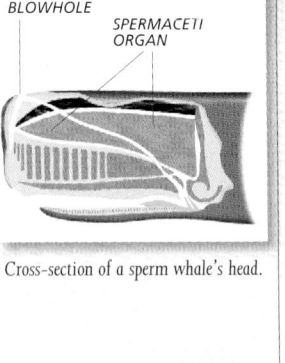

BLOWHOLE SPERMACETI ORGAN

Cross-section of a sperm whale's head.

motion, lasting non-stop until today. Various nations would become a part of this enterprise. The exact size of the total sperm whale stock in the world is not known today, but optimists assume that there are over 2,000,000 animals; others believe the figure is closer to 1,500,000. Also, about half of them are believed to be in the North Pacific. After whale surveys off Iceland in 1987 and 1989, experts think that about

In November 1861 off Tenerife in the Canary Islands, the crew of the French corvette Alecton harpooned a giant squid. However, they only managed to get the top part of the animal, the tail, onboard. Not until 12 years later did science acquire its first giant squid for exhaustive research.

1,400 animals, on average, frequent the ocean around Iceland.

Sperm whales, more commonly than other species, strand on beaches and die. This happens in Iceland, for example, practically every year. This picture was taken after such an incident that occurred on 25 January 1992, in Thykkvibær (S-Iceland). The owner of the Dísukot farm, Kristinn Markússon, stands next to the 12- to 14-metre long whale. In previous centuries, sperm whale teeth were in great demand by craftsmen. A trace of this demand seems to remain because, if you look closely, you will see that all of the animal's lower jaw has been removed.

bowhead whale
Balaena mysticetus

 The bowhead whale belongs to the suborder of baleen whales (Mysticeti), the family of *Balaenidae* and, finally, the genus *Balaena*.

The bowhead whale's body, like the right whale's, is mostly black or dark. However, the forward part of the lower jaw is white. Likewise, the tail stock is light on its sides and underside. There is no dorsal fin, but the whale has large flippers, not very long, but wide and round. The flukes are also enormous.

There is more worth noting about this unusually large whale. Its head, for example, is more than one-third of its total length, and its jaw is larger still than the right whale's.

Also, its tongue, no small appendage, weighs about two tons. Its baleens, 230 to 360 in number, are dark-grey or black and are located on both sides of the animal's upper jaw. They are the longest of any whale's, measuring 4.3 m. The whale's blow can reach a height of 6 m.

The bowhead whale is an animal of the far North and much more willing to go into cold waters than its relative, the right whale. The whale's habitat is the polar seas of the North. As protection against the cold, the whale has, on the one hand, unusually thick skin (about 2.5 cm) and, on the other hand, an enormous layer of blubber. Specimens of this animal have been caught where the layer of blubber was 60 cm or even more.

The bowhead whale's main diet is plankton, especially krill, although it also consumes calanus. Its fishing method, unlike that of the rorquals, is to swim

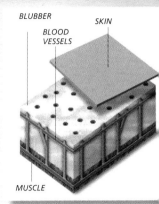

Cross-section of skin and blubber. Whalers regarded the bowhead and right whales as "right" whales because due to the thick layer of blubber they carried, they floated when shot, and also because of how slowly they usually swam. Rorquals, on the other hand, sank. It was not until the Norwegian Svend Foyn redesigned the expanding harpoon that things changed.

with its maw open at a shallow depth until it has collected enough to swallow. The right whale employs the same method. The rorquals, however,

On the lookout for whales. The person on watch got a fixed percentage for each spotted and caught whale.

been observed rooting in bottom silt down to a depth of 30 m in order to flush up small animals hiding there. The bowhead whale is a very slow swimmer, moving along at only 2 to 7 km per hour on long journeys.

Very little else is known about this species, especially because of the geographical difficulty of approaching it for research. Experts, however, believe that males mature sexually upon reaching a length of 11.5 m, while the females have to reach a length of 13 or 14 m. Mating is believed to occur in March and pregnancy to take about 12 to 16 months. Calves, which are born in mid-winter on the southern edge of the whale's distribution area (around the Arctic Circle), are about 4 m long when new-born. They nurse for about one year. Births of twins may occur occasionally. Fully grown females are thought to bear

The bowhead whale was the main whale hunted by the Dutch in the 17th century. It was caught east of Greenland and off Svalbard. Estimates state that up to 100,000 animals were killed there. The animals' blubber, from which oil was rendered, was especially in demand along with the baleen that were used in the the manufacture of gentlewomen's corsets and crinolines.

young every 2 to 7 years.

Scientists think that there are five separate stocks of bowhead whale. One inhabits the Bering Sea, the Chukchi and Beaufort Seas. Another lives in the Sea of Okhotsk, the third in the Davis Strait and Baffin Bay, the fourth in Hudson Bay and the fifth in the Greenland Sea and Barents Sea.

In the 17th century, Dutch

Nowadays, after the bowhead whale was protected, its principal enemy is the killer whale. In West Greenland, people once witnessed a deathly-frightened bowhead whale swim up on the beach to get away from this enemy. It did, however, manage to kill one of them with its flukes. This old watercolour painting shows killer whales attacking a bowhead whale.

with the exception of the sei whale, fill their maw with sea-water and swallow whatever is caught. Sometimes, the bow-head whale also feeds at some depth, and these animals have

whalers hunted the bowhead whale most of all. It was taken east of Greenland. Later, after the above-mentioned area was exhausted, people sought the animals elsewhere, finding them west of Greenland, and history repeated itself. Scots and people from the United States were the primary agents then.

In 1946, the bowhead whale was protected, except that Inuits were permitted to hunt a few animals for their livelihood.

right whale
Eubalaena glacialis

 The right whale belongs to the suborder of baleen whales (Mysticeti) and the family of Balaenidae. Then, finally it is in the genus Eubalaena. This whale's body is round, spindle-shaped and tending toward stoutness. The circumference, where the whale is largest, is about 60% of its length.

The whale's head is large, accounting for about one-third of the animal's total length.

From the snout to the blowholes, there is a row of coarse growths, often called callosities. The same kind of growths form over the eyes and on the sides of the lower jaw. The function of the growths is not known, but most experts believe they are more of an annoyance to the animal than anything else

since they provide perfect conditions for the growth of barnacles and other parasites. Among other things, lice species found nowhere else make their home in these horny outgrowths. In addition to the callosities, the snout has a few locks of hair, both on the upper and lower jaws.

The right whale's mouth is enormous and so structured that the animal can never close it completely. 220 to 260 dark to black baleen plates hang from both sides of the upper jaw (totally 440 to 520). They can be up to 2.8 m long. The whale's tongue is also gargantuan, weighing 1.5 tons.

The right whale's predominant colour is black, which sometimes approaches brown tones. However, toward the rear on the underbelly around the animal's sexual organs and rectal opening, there are, in addition, often white patches. Also, in

certain seasons, the skin on the backs of some animals flakes, so that they become white-speckled.

The right whale has no dorsal fin. The unavoidable consequence is that it usually swims very slowly, paddling along at 4 to 7 km per hour maximum.

The right whale's flippers are quite long, wide and round. Its flukes are also huge, with a prominent notch in the middle.

As is usual with baleen whales, there are two blowholes, as opposed to the single blowhole of toothed whales. When the right whale blows, two vapour columns go up, one on each side, forming a "V", reaching as high as five metres.

The right whale's main diet is plankton, especially krill, although it also feeds on calanus. Unlike the rorquals, the right whale's feeding method

is to swim with its maw open, sometimes along the surface of the ocean, although usually below the surface or along the bottom, until it has collected enough to swallow. Scientists believe that a fully grown right whale requires 1 to 2.5 tons of feed per day to live and thrive. Disputes have been long-standing about how the various extant right whale stocks should be defined. Some want to regard them as a single species, Eubalaena glacialis, with three variations (glacialis in the Northern Hemisphere, australis in the Southern Hemisphere and japonica in the Sea of Japan). Others prefer to see them as two independent species (E. glacialis, in the Northern Hemisphere, and E. australis in the Southern Hemisphere), while still others see them as three independent species (adding, then, the right whale in the Sea of Japan, E. japonica). A ruling on these differing

views will probably be a long time coming, but in this book, the first alternative is chosen and followed.

Some treatises classify the right whale under the genus Balaena, like the bowhead whale, and not under Eubalaena as is done here. The same applies to these speculations as to those mentioned above.

Long ago, the right whale was common in many areas, except in the warmest waters. However, because of the heavy hunting of the stocks since the 11th century, not many right whales remain. This whale was first annihilated in the Bay of Biscay, but then people, mostly Basques and Dutchmen, came to the North, after having exhausted the stocks further south, and continued to hunt the whale. By about 1700, the stock had nearly collapsed in the eastern part of the Atlantic, with the same thing happening off

North America around 1800. In the 19th century alone, about 100,000 animals were killed. The right whale was universally protected in 1935.

Whether the right whale stock can recover is uncertain. Because of the low number of right whales in the oceans, it is very difficult to do research on its migrations and life cycle. Nearly nothing, for example, is known of its migratory routes. On the other hand, females are believed to bear young every 2 to 4 years, with the term of pregnancy being 10 to 12 months. New-born calves nurse for 4 to 8 months. They probably mature sexually at 7 to 15 years of age, at least in the case of females.

Nothing is known about their internal group organisation except that the link between mothers and their offspring is very strong and close.

gray whale
Eschrichtius robustus

The Gray whale belongs to the suborder of baleen whales (Mysticeti), the family of Eschrichtidae and finally the genus Eschrichtius.

In 1640, the Icelander, Jón Gudmundsson the Learned, wrote an essay on the natural sciences, titled A Short Instruction on Iceland's Diverse Nature, which was later usually shortened for convenience to On Iceland's Diverse Nature. Gudmundsson had good relations with the Basques who engaged in whaling off Iceland in the 17th century, and the descriptions and drawings in his essay bear clear witness to firsthand knowledge of whales. There, among other things, he describes one species of whale that he calls "sandlægja" (one who lies in the sand). This is an animal name used in the Snorra-Edda.

Gudmundsson's description seems to indicate clearly that the species involved was the Gray whale, and that this species inhabited the North Atlantic in previous centuries, but became extinct there in the 17th or 18th century because, today, it is found only in the North Pacific Ocean.

In all likelihood, an English natural scientist was the first to publish a precise description of this whale in 1725. There it is called "scrag".

In 1864, the English zoologist Gray classified the whale under a special family that he called Eschrichtidae in honour of Daniel Frederick Eschricht, a professor of zoology in Copenhagen. The reason for classifying it under a special family had to do with various biological peculiarities of the species. In short, the shape of the whale's body seemed to fall between that of a right whale and a rorqual. For example, like the right whale,

The famous Gray whale picture by Jón Gudmundsson the Learned, from 1640.

the Gray whale lacks a dorsal fin. However, it has a strange outgrowth on its tail stock like a row of bumps, not unlike the humpback whale. Also, although it does not have real throat grooves or stretch marks on its throat and underbelly like the rorquals, a trace of such grooves is discernible under its "chin".

The Gray whale is grey, but because of the parasites infesting the whale, and also because the skin loses its colour over time, the original colour becomes blotched with yellow or white.

This happens especially on the head, around the blowhole and on the back. Fully grown males are, on average, 11 to 14 m long and weigh 16 tons, while females are slightly larger, 11 to 15 m long and weighing 30 to 35 tons.

The body is long and relatively thin. The flippers are short and broad, tapering at the ends. The flukes are large. The head is thin in front, ending nearly in a point. The baleens, hanging down from both sides of the upper jaw, number 260 to 360 and are very fine and small (at any rate, compared with those in other baleen whales). The underbelly grooves, numbering only 2 to 5, are short and deep. On the top of the snout, there are clumps where various parasites, lice, barnacles and even seaweed easily settle in to live and thrive.

The Gray whale is migratory, as is common with baleen whales and many others. It migrates north in the summer and back south in the winter into warmer waters. Mating occurs over a three-week period from late November to

Whale lice.

GILLS

early December when the animals are on the way south. Pregnancy lasts for 13 to 14 months. New-born calves are nearly 5 m long and weigh about 500 kg. Gray whales mature sexually at eight years, by then having grown to 11 or 12 m. They do not attain their full length until 40 years of age.

Various sources, including the above-mentioned essay on natural science by Jón the Learned, clearly indicate that long ago, there were three Gray whale stocks in the world. One inhabited the North Atlantic, both off Iceland and the other Nordic countries, and was also off the British Isles and in the surrounding waters. Another, which the Koreans hunted heavily until 1966 and nearly exterminated, was in the North-west Pacific Ocean. The third was in the North-east Pacific in the area from California north to Alaska. Nowadays, there are

only two stocks because the North Atlantic stock died out in the 17th century, as mentioned above, without any organised hunting. Without doubt, however, the whale's tendency to approach coasts and even go into river mouths and shallow bays accelerated its extinction. In addition, the whale is a slow swimmer and unsuspicious, at least if left unmolested.

In the North Pacific, there were great numbers of this whale. Heavy hunting of it began in the 19th century, lasting far into the 20th century. Thus, it was nearly exterminated there, too. However, before this happened, conservationist associations in the United States took strict measures. The most remarkable thing was that the Gray whale reacted worse than other whales when people followed it, transforming into a fierce creature that was nicknamed the "devil fish".

Today, the world stock of Gray whale is clearly recovering. The biggest increase is in the North-east Pacific, where the largest number of extant Gray whales is some 15,000 to 24,700 animals. Their summer habitation is in the North off the coast of Alaska. When winter starts, they migrate south, all the way to California and Mexico. This seasonal migration is one of the most massive in the animal kingdom. Every 12 months, that is, in making the roundtrip from the polar seas south to warmer waters and back, the whales have to go more than 20,000 km. The latest research indicates that only the humpback whale migrates farther.

Because of the poor condition of the Gray whale stock mentioned above, scientists have monitored developments closely. One consequence has been that more is known of this baleen

whale than of any other extant whale species.

Undoubtedly this whale's tame and calm nature also aided these efforts. As mentioned above, the whale is practically man-loving and keeps to the shallows, not the open ocean, as do many of the baleen whales that are less well known. Gray whales are most commonly in groups of a few animals (1 to 3, on average). Groups of up to 16 have, on occasion, been observed. If, on the other hand, conditions on feeding grounds are very good, several hundred animals may gather in an area of a few square kilometres. The relations between individuals then are rather loose and free-floating. That is, they are really many small groups in close proximity.

The Gray whale is unlike other baleen whales in that it hunts its food only on the bottom of the sea, not in the upper layers or on the surface of the ocean. Its fishing method is to drive its lower jaw into a soft bottom and swim forward, thus churning up small animals lying hidden there.

On long journeys, these whales swim at an average of 8 km per hour, but can reach a speed of 20 km per hour, if necessary. On long journeys, however, although this speed of 8 km per hour is held pretty steady, they come to the surface every three or four minutes to blow three to five times. The blow reaches a height of three to four metres.

In the Pacific Ocean, other than the eastern part, the animals have a difficult time. The stock in the North-west Pacific is, for example, believed to be no more than 200 to 300 animals, or even only 100 to 200. Understandably, the Gray whale is therefore still protected. However, the Eskimos of Alaska and Siberia may catch a few animals per year for their livelihood.

In its own habitat, this whale species is greatly threatened by killer whales, especially during migrations. Likewise, in the summer, sharks are believed to be a major threat, especially to young calves.

humpback whale
Megaptera novaeangliae

The humpback whale belongs to the sub-order of baleen whales (*Mysticeti*) and the family of rorqual whales (*Balaenopteridae*), but is so unlike them in many ways that it is appointed to the subfamily *Megapterinae* and finally to the genus *Megaptera*, of which it is the sole member.

Most commonly, the humpback whale is black or dark-grey on its back and sides, but white or grey on its underbelly. The colour pattern on its throat and chest can vary from one animal to another. The flippers are generally black on top and white on the tips and underside. Certain stocks of humpback whale, however, have flippers that are almost completely white. They are one of the humpback whale's characteristics and can grow to a length

NÁTTÚRUVERKUR

The male humpback whale is regarded as the greatest singer in the whale kingdom. The sounds that can travel a long distance underwater, even many hundreds of kilometres, are very diverse and complex and are not the same from animals in the Atlantic on the one hand and the Pacific Ocean on the other hand. They change slightly from year to year. The purpose of these songs is not known, but they can last for several hours at a time or even days.

This picture, which appeared in the May edition of the magazine Náttúruverkur in 1979, says a great deal. In fact, it portrays the two kinds of attitudes toward whales being discussed at this time. People come either to watch them or to kill them. Which will prevail?

of 5 m and a breadth of 1 m. There are various hypotheses as to why the animal has developed such wondrous appendages as these. One is that they work like a cooling apparatus in warm seas, as a dog's tongue does on land. Another is that they increase the beast's nimbleness, facilitating the rotund body's manoeuvrings through the sea.

The flukes are also enormous, split in the centre and often very

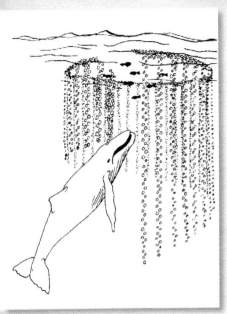

One of the humpback whale's fishing methods is to dive beneath a shoal and swim around it, releasing air bubbles that act as a net and then attacking.

ragged. The colour of the under-surface can vary greatly by individual, sometimes being completely dark, but most commonly it is light-coloured or whitish.

A fully grown humpback whale is from 11 to 15 m long, weighing about 25 to 30 tons, on average. Experts believe that the whale's maximum length is 18 m. Females are a bit larger than males.

Like other rorqual whales, the humpback whale has grooves on its chest and sides, though fewer than its relatives do, generally only 14 to 35 in number, but much broader and coarser. The dorsal fin is also rather small and situated much farther forward than it is on other species, just aft of the centre. The fin's shape varies from broad and triangular to narrow and crescent-shaped and everything in between. This shape variability of the dorsal fin previously caused scientists to speculate that there were actually many dissimilar species. Most now agree, however, that all humpback whales are the same species, but that there are at least 10 regional variations of the stock, dissimilar in many ways as to behaviour and appearance.

The humpback whale has 740 to 800 baleens on both sides of the upper jaw. Most of them are relatively short and dark-grey in colour, but with black edges. On the head or snout are three rows of knobs. There are knobs on the lower jaw as well, and these can also be found on the forward edge of the flippers. Barnacles and parasites often infest the knobs. The tail stock is also covered with knobs up to the dorsal fin, not unlike the sperm whale.

Because of its ballooning lines, the humpback whale cannot swim as fast as other rorqual whales, despite its enormous flippers (if the above theory is correct) and, on average, moves slowly at from 5 to 10 km per hour. It can nevertheless sprint at up to 27 km per hour, if aroused.

The humpback whale is migratory, as are other rorqual whales. It makes seasonal swings between cold seas and the equator. In the summer, it travels to cold waters in both hemispheres to utilise the plankton or krill that are found there in great quantity, but in the winter, the humpback whale migrates to equatorial waters to mate and give birth. In the North Atlantic, the southern boundary of the whale's distribution is off North-western Africa and the West Indies, and its northern boundary is the edge of the polar ice cap. However, a few animals stay off Iceland all year.

In the North Atlantic, the animals mate on their way north, usually in March and April. A pregnancy lasts 11 months, with females giving birth every two or three years. Calves are then born in February or March. They nurse for 6 to 10 months, doubling in length to 8 or 9 m. Experts believe that humpback whales mature sexually at about five years of age, at which time they have reached a length of 12 m. Humpback whales often travel alone or in small groups of 2 to 5 animals when they are feeding in the polar oceans. However, when they return to equatorial waters in the winter, relations become considerably more complex, being very much based on sexual and pregnancy cycles.

The humpback whale's main food is krill, but it also consumes a large quantity of small pelagic fish species, such as herring, capelin and mackerel, when available, and sandeel. In recent years, an increasing number of whales has been noticed on Icelandic fishing grounds. They follow the capelin migrations from the West Fjords to the East of the country, often making life very difficult for the capelin ships. Ships have even had to stop fishing because frequently, after casting, up to five humpback whales get caught in the net, tearing and rupturing it to free themselves. One capelin net costs ISK 20 million (approximately US$ 282,000), and such damage is not compensated by the insurance companies.

The whales usually catch their food between the surface and a depth of 50 m. The fishing method is similar to that of other rorqual whales: they take a mouthful of water and swallow whatever they can filter from it. However, the humpback whale is different from the rest of the family in that it often fishes co-operatively. A favourite method is to swim under a shoal and release air that provides concealment. The whales then rush up with open maws. Another related technique is to dive beneath a shoal and swim around it, releasing air bubbles that act as a net, collecting the fish into a compact group and then attacking.

In previous centuries, whalers did not especially seek out humpback whales, but hunted them more on a random, individual basis. However, at the turn of the century, they began to show more interest in the species. Then, whaling fleets, especially from Norway, killed off nearly the entire humpback whale stock in the North Atlantic. Elsewhere, the same thing happened to humpback whale stocks. For example, from 1900 to 1940, over 100,000 animals were killed in the Southern Hemisphere and about 50,000 more from 1940 to 1963.

A preservation movement began in 1938 when just a fraction of the stock was left in the ocean deeps. The humpback whale was universally protected in the North Atlantic in 1956, in the Southern Hemisphere in 1963 and in the North Pacific in 1966.

blue whale
Balaenoptera musculus

The blue whale belongs to the suborder of baleen whales (Mysticeti) and the family of rorquals (Balaenopteridae). Then, it is in the subfamily Balaenopterinae and finally in the genus Balaenoptera.

It is generally regarded as the largest animal ever to have lived on the earth.

Today, the fully grown blue whale is "no more than" 25 to 27 m long, on average, and weighs about 110 to 130 tons. In former times, these figures could be much higher. In 1909, a female more than 33 m long was caught and brought to a whaling station in South Georgia in the United States. The weight of the colossus is not known, but in 1947 another female was caught that was about 7 m shorter, and it weighed some 190 tons, that is, 80 tons more than what is generally believed to be the average weight today.

The blue whale, like other rorquals, has an extremely slender and supple build, oblong and thin. It is mostly dark-grey or blue-grey all over with some light mottling on the sides. The head is relatively small and flat and the flippers long and narrow and, in fact, white underneath. The dorsal fin, which is small, being only 30 cm high, is situated far back on the body and has various shapes. The flukes are, on the other hand, huge, broad and very powerful. Females are a bit larger than males. On the underside from the neck back to the navel, the whale has 55 to 68 hollows or furrows, enabling it to expand its underbelly if necessary. These throat grooves are one of a rorqual's characteristics.

Baleen whales have no teeth. Instead, they have an extremely powerful fishing apparatus, a kind of sieve, called baleen plates. They comprise many rows of thin, oblong plates of horn that hang down from both sides of the upper gums. The number and length of these plates vary by species. The blue whale has 520 to 800 of them, all black and relatively small, compared with what other baleen whales have.

The blue whale migrates with the seasons. In the spring, it journeys a vast distance north to the edge of the polar ice to feed and fatten itself. Then, when the season turns colder, it migrates south again to the equator and warmer waters where it feeds very little, if at all, for 5 to 6 months.

The animals mate from May to September, with most of the mating taking place at the height of summer. Pregnancy lasts 10 to 11 months. Calves are generally born in the spring when the animals are migrating to their feeding grounds. When the calf stops nursing at 8 months, it has more than doubled its length (15 m) and increased its weight tenfold (25 tons). This is equivalent to gaining 90 kg per day. The whale is thought to mature sexually at about the age of 10. Females bear young every two or three years.

Long ago, whalers told stories of interbreeding between blue whales and fin whales. For years, these reports were variously believed, but in 1983, this was confirmed when a rorqual male with the appearance of a crossbreed of the two species washed ashore. It proved to be sterile. In 1986, a female rorqual was caught south-west of Iceland. Its dorsal fin was similar to a fin whale's, but its baleen plates and the colour of its underbelly were that of a blue whale. The animal carried a foetus. A genetic analysis showed that the animal's mother was a blue whale and its father a fin whale. The foetus's father, on the other hand, was a blue whale. In 1989, a third crossbreed was caught that was sterile.

The blue whale's diet is mostly krill, a small crustacean resembling shrimp. It also hunts small, schooling fish and even squid and octopus. The whale blows 8 to 15 times before diving. Its dives last 10 to 15 minutes, on average, and reach a depth of 50 to 100 m. Its fishing method is to fill its maw with sea teeming with krill, expel the water and swallow whatever is left. Experts say that the animal can consume up to 8 tons of krill per day. This rorqual's blow of up to 12 m is also an indication of its incredible size and power.

The blue whale is a creature of the high seas, rather shy, and is often alone when travelling or together with 2 or 3 other animals. When fishing, it cruises

The blue whale today is "no more" than 25 to 27 m long, on average, fully grown and weighs about 100 to 130 tons. Years ago, however, these figures were higher. By extrapolating from this or comparing it with other species, as done above, where on the one hand, are elephants and, on the other, steers, it can be more easily seen how enormously heavy the blue whale is.

at 2 to 6.5 km per hour, but on long trips its speed is 5 to 14 km per hour. If the animal is fleeing something, it can reach speeds of 30 km per hour.

The blue whale is distributed throughout the world's oceans. Previously, experts thought there were three main stocks: one in the North Pacific Ocean, another in the North Atlantic and a third in the Southern Hemisphere.

Now, however, it is more common to talk of three sub-species. One is in the Northern Hemisphere, B. m. musculus (in the North Pacific and North Atlantic Oceans). Two others are in the Southern Hemisphere, B. m. intermedia, on the one hand (bigger than the other two), and B. m. brevicauda, on the other (by far the smallest, it was previously called the dwarf blue whale), which is found only in the Indian Ocean and South-east Atlantic Ocean.

The blue whale, to put it mildly, has come off very poorly in its struggle with mankind in all ocean areas. After excessive hunting by the Norwegians and Icelanders in the northern oceans, it was finally protected in 1960 and, then, in 1965, all over the world. The results of surveys done off Iceland indicate that the stock has a long way to go before becoming as strong as it was before 1900 when whaling was at its peak.

However, the whale is in no danger of becoming extinct. The figure 1,000 has been mentioned in this regard, with 1,500 animals in all being in the whole North Atlantic. When the stock was strongest, the first whales came to East and West Iceland from the southern seas in April, with the main migrations occurring from May to June. The whales were dispersed all around the country. How the migrations are today is uncertain.

In the 19th century, before the hunting began that nearly wiped the species out, the world stock is estimated to have been about 300,000 animals. Nowadays, however, experts' most generous estimates are approximately 14,000 animals. Others mention lower figures of 9,000 or even 6,000.

Excluding man, the blue whale has no natural enemies except for the killer whale that is known to have attacked and killed various large whales. This is the exception, however, rather than the rule.

Finally, the blue whale is believed to live at least to the age of 100.

fin whale
Balaenoptera physalus

The fin whale belongs to the suborder of baleen whales (Mysticeti), the family of Balaenopteridae, the subfamily of Balaenopterina and the genus Balaenoptera.

It is regarded as the next largest of all whales. In the Southern Hemisphere, the length of fully grown animals is 24 to 26 m and the weight about 80 tons, but in the Northern Hemisphere, these figures are much lower. Off Iceland, the males, for example, are about 18 m long, on average, and females approximately 19.5 m. The longest animals off Iceland reach a length of 22 m. Easily distinguished from the blue whale, the fin whale is dark grey on top and white underneath, with a clear division between the colours on the animal's sides. Also, the animal has peculiarly asymmetrical patches on the sides of its head, so that the right side of the jaw is light-yellow or white, and the left side black. Its head is more tapered and sharper at the nose than the blue whale's, and there is a singular, oblong ridge along the top.

The flippers are long and narrow, the dorsal fin relatively tall (about 60 cm), and the tail stock is thin and even flimsy-looking along the sides. The baleens are usually white or lead-grey. Hanging down from both sides of the upper jaw, they number 520 to 960 in all, more than the blue whale has. The baleens can be up to 72 cm long and 30 cm wide. The whale's blow can reach a height of 4 to 6 m.

For the most part, the fin whale is an open-ocean whale, preferring the polar seas and colder areas. It is a migratory whale, staying in warm waters in the winter, generally from

November to January, where the animals mate and bear young. The term of pregnancy is about 12 months, and a new-born calf is 6 to 6.5 m long and weighs 1.5 to 2 tons. It nurses for at least 6 to 8 months, doubling in length in this period and reaching a weight of more than 13 tons. The whale matures sexually when 6 to 12 years old and grows to its full length at age 15.

Long ago, whalers told stories of interbreeding between blue whales and fin whales, as is mentioned also in the section on blue whales. For years, these reports were variously believed, but in 1983, this was confirmed when a rorqual male with the appearance of a crossbreed of the two species washed ashore. It proved to be sterile. In 1986, a female rorqual was caught south-west of Iceland. Its dorsal fin was similar to a fin whale's, but its baleen plates and the

Marine biologists think that the small and large whales on Iceland's fishing banks and in the nearby ocean areas consume about 4.5 million tons annually. The mainstay of the baleen whales' diet are relatively small, free-floating crustaceans (especially Euphausiacea), about 80 species, the length of some of which can be up to 5 cm. There are also calanus species (Copepoda) that are still smaller, their length not exceeding a few millimetres. All the species are called krill. The picture is of the Euphausiacea. Toothed whales, on the other hand, primarily eat fish.

colour of its underbelly were that of a blue whale. The animal carried a foetus. A genetic analysis showed that the animal's mother was a blue whale and its father a fin whale. The foetus's father, on the other hand, was a blue whale. In 1989, a third crossbreed was caught that was sterile.

After the period of mating and giving birth, the fin whales journey again to colder waters, even ranging as far as the edge of the polar ice. They gather in clusters in the best krill areas. The main, large groups, usually called stocks, number seven in the North Atlantic. They are: 1) the East Greenland-Iceland stock, 2) the Northern Norway stock, 3) the West Norway-Faeroe Islands stock, 4) the Spain-Portugal-British Isles stock, 5) the West Greenland stock, 6) the Newfoundland-Labrador stock and 7) the Nova Scotia stock.

Experts believe that the fin whale takes little nourishment at its wintering grounds and is therefore very lean when it arrives at its summer locations. The whale's main diet is plankton, but it also consumes various small, pelagic schooling fish, especially around the time of migration, for example, herring and capelin. In other ocean areas, squid and octopus are added to this list. The fin whale usually swims on its side when gathering food, a manoeuvre believed to facilitate the closing of its gigantic jaws. It dives down to 300 m in search of prey and can stay down for 10 to 15 minutes at a time. This is longer than the blue whale usually stays down.

The fin whale is by far the commonest species of large whale found off Iceland. The first animals arrive in the North from southern waters in March, but it is not until in May and the beginning of June that the main migration arrives. Surveys have found the greatest numbers of fin whales off West Iceland, near the edge of the continental shelf and, also, considerable numbers off East Greenland and

in the area far to the south-west of Iceland. This stock is called the East Greenland-Iceland stock, which has always been the nation's main whaling stock. The fin whale, like the blue whale, has fared poorly in its contact with humankind. However, hunting of the whale had to await the coming of the modern whaling ship, that is, steamboats, which were fast enough to follow this champion swimmer. The fin whale is believed capable of swimming at a speed of 35 km per hour and cruising up to 300 km in a day. In the middle of this century, approximately 30,000 animals were killed world-wide, most of them in the Southern Hemisphere. In 1976, hunting was discontinued there as well as in the North Pacific Ocean. In the Northern Hemisphere, the Norwegians, more than any other nation, hunted the fin whale and, for the most part, exterminated the stock off their own shores over a 40-year period, from 1850 to the turn of the century. Hunting of the fin whale off Iceland began in 1883 and reached a peak in 1904 when 562 animals were killed. After this, fin-whale hunting began to decline. In 1913, the Althingi (Icelandic Parliament) put an end to this hunting by enacting a law banning all whale hunting after 1915. This ban lasted only 14 years, until 1929. Then, the Norwegians returned and hunted the fin whale until 1937. Icelanders began modern whaling in 1935, continuing until 1939. After the end of the Second World War (1948), they resumed whaling until 1989, although only for scientific purposes the last few years. From the start, the fin whale was the mainstay of the catch with, on average, 236 animals per year being caught from 1948 to 1984. This is nearly 90% of the total number of whales caught.

sei whale
Balaenoptera borealis

The sei whale belongs to the suborder of baleen whales (*Mysticeti*), the family of rorquals (*Balaenopteridae*) and the subfamily of *Balaenopterinae*. Then, it is in the genus *Balaenoptera*.

Of the rorquals off Iceland's coasts, least is known about the sei whale. It is about 10% smaller in the Northern Hemisphere than in the Southern.

The sei whale is dark-grey or almost black on top and on the entire tail stock and flippers. The underbelly is light-coloured. There are also light patches here and there all over its body, along with spots on its head. This whale is very similar to other rorquals in shape, long and slender, although perhaps not as thin as the fin whale, and the sei whale's head is rounder. Also, its dorsal fin is twice as high, being about 60 cm. Furthermore, it is crescent-shaped and situated farther forward. The flukes and flippers are dark underneath, while on the fin whale they are whitish. Finally, the throat grooves on the sei whale, about 38 to 60 in number, do not reach as far back as they do on the fin whale. On both sides of the upper jaw, the sei whale has 318 to 340 black baleen plates that can be up to 78 cm long. As with other baleen whales, the sei whale's main diet is plankton. Off Iceland, it consumes krill almost exclusively, which is also the main diet of the blue and fin whales. In other oceans, however, calanus is also an important food source. In addition, the sei whale also hunts considerable quantities of pelagic, schooling fish species along with squid and octopus. Thus, this species is more opportunistic than its relatives or less set in its ways, taking whatever is available at the time. The whale swims rather slowly, on average, or at about 2 to 6.5 km per hour, while hunting food, and 5 to 14 km per hour when migrating. However, if necessary, it can go much faster, even surpassing the fin whale, some say. Not much of the whale is visible when it swims on the surface, and its diving is also very inconspicuous, the flukes not even lifting out of the water. On a dive, it can stay down up to 20 minutes and probably goes no deeper than 300 m. Its blow is small, an expanding column, just a bit lower than the fin whale's. The sei whale is found in all oceans of the world, except perhaps in the coldest waters of both hemispheres. It likes best to be in waters of 8° to 25°C. Only the biggest and most powerful individuals go into the polar seas and, then, only in mid- or late summer. Like other rorquals, the sei whale migrates toward the equator in late autumn, or in October-November, and stays for the winter. Sei whales travel generally in pods of 3 to 5, although larger shoals have been observed, that is, of 50 or more animals. There is some division according to gender, age, etc. Mating takes place from November to February, and pregnancy lasts for about 12 months. A new-born calf nurses until 6 to 7 months of age. At that time, it has grown to a length of 8 m and weighs about four tons. It matures sexually at 8 to 11 years of age and attains full growth when 12 years old. The females bear young every two years.

The sei whale is most commonly seen off Iceland in August and September, usually in the deep waters between Iceland and Greenland. However, it rarely goes into the cold waters north and east of the country. The whale surveys in 1989

The picture shows a cross-section of a rorqual head (left) and a right whale (right). The view is of the front of the animals.

indicated that about 10,500 animals were south and east of the country, especially, though, between Iceland and Greenland and south from there.

A living sei whale is very seldom found stranded on a beach since it is a deep-sea whale and is seldom seen near shore. Some occasionally do wash up, usually individuals that have died on the high seas and have been borne to land by currents. There are no known instances of multiple strandings.

The sei whale has not benefited from its contact with human-

When the maw is filled with krill, the animals press their tongues to the roofs of their mouths, forcing out the sea water. The krill, however, cannot escape, but are caught by the baleen and swallowed. This is the most efficient food gathering known in the whole animal kingdom.

kind, even though it was never hunted as a primary whale. Rather, it was used as a back-up when something else did not work out. The number of animals caught always varied. For example, in 1968 no sei whales were caught off Iceland, while in 1971, 240 animals were taken. The reason for this is that sei whale migration to Iceland and, in fact, to Norway usually is very irregular, and no explanation of the phenomenon is known. However, despite irregular catching of the species, its stocks began to suffer so

much depletion that preventive measures had to be taken. In 1979, a comprehensive ban on whaling was set for the species, with the exception of felling 85 animals per year. Since 1986, several animals have been taken annually for scientific purposes, from 10 to 40.

The stocks in the Northern Hemisphere have not yet been successfully differentiated, but for convenience specialists refer to the so-called Iceland-Greenland stock, whose distribution is south to the mid-North Atlantic. On the other hand, experts believe that there are three stocks in the Northern Pacific Ocean: an eastern stock, a central stock and a western stock. The stocks in the Northern and Southern Hemispheres are thought not to intermingle.

minke whale
Balaenoptera acutorostrata

 The minke whale belongs to the suborder of baleen whales (Mysticeti), the family of rorqual whales (Balaenopteridae), the subfamily Balaenopterinae and, finally, the genus of Balaenoptera.

The minke whale is similar to other rorquals in shape, but it is by far the smallest, seldom reaching a length of more than 9 m. Nevertheless, minke whales of 11 m have been found. In the Southern Hemisphere, the fully grown males are, on average, 8 m long, while the females are just over that, about 8.2 m. They seldom weigh more than 8 tons. Minke whales in the Northern Hemisphere run a bit smaller than this.

The minke whale is dark-grey or almost black on its back and sides and white on the under-

belly. The dorsal fin is relatively high for a rorqual, sweeping slightly back or crescent-shaped. The flippers are rather long and thin, their length being 12% of the animal's total length, and the flukes are large and broad. They do not usually come out of the water when the animal dives.

The baleens number from 230 to 360, being 300 on average. They hang down from the upper jaw on both sides and are a creamy-yellow colour in the front, but progressively darker farther back. Their maximum length is 30 cm.

The grooves in the underbelly number 50 to 70.

The white strip or belt running across the flippers has always been considered one of the species' main identifying features. However, the matter is not so simple because many minke whales off the South Pole do not have this white patterning. The blow is generally 2 to 3 m high and is discernible only in the most favourable weather conditions. The minke whale is chiefly a coastal whale, often travelling very close to land, especially the females.

The species is distributed throughout all the world's oceans. Previously, experts believed that there were three main stocks, one in the North Atlantic, another in the North Pacific and a third in the South Pacific. It was considered unlikely that they mixed with each other. Now, however, experts speak more often of three subspecies: *B. a. acutorostrata* (North Atlantic), *B. a. davidsonii* (North Pacific), og *B. a. bonarensis* (Southern Hemisphere).

The minke whale's distribution in the North Atlantic reaches from the edge of the polar ice in the North south to Cape Hatteras in North America and the Mediterranean

The Japanese have been avid consumers of whale meat for a long time, as can be seen in this old advertisement.

Sea. In the winter, the animals stay, for the most part, south of 50° N. The minke whale is very common all around Iceland in the summer, but was only hunted west and north of the country when hunting was practiced and permitted.

The minke whale is exceptionally curious, unlike other rorquals, especially when young. It is quite willing to approach ships and boats. Approximately one-fifth of the animals caught by the Norwegians approach the boats in this way. The minke whale can be very sportive, breaching high into the air and coming head-down, rakish and lithe like a dolphin, or on its side or back, like the humpback whale, with the accompanying tumult and splashes.

The minke whale is migratory, in the autumn seeking the equator and, in the spring, the poles. On each leg of the journey, the whale often travels 9,000 km in these endeavours.

The animals mate in their winter location from January to May. Pregnancy lasts 10 to 12 months, with births occurring from November to March The calf nurses for only four months, until it reaches 4.5 m. It matures sexually at six or seven years of age.

The main food of minke whale in the Southern Hemisphere is plankton or krill and also squid and octopus. Animals in the Northern Hemisphere, however, prefer small schooling fish, especially herring, cod, capelin and sandeel.

Minke whales prefer to travel alone or in groups of two to three animals, swimming at speeds of 24 to 30 km per hour. It is rare to find a larger group except at their summer feeding grounds. In the Southern Hemisphere, however, there have been instances of 100 animals in a shoal.

Through the years, this species has been utilised for food as much as possible in all oceans of the world. It would take too long to tell the whole story here, but, briefly, over a 50-year period from 1920 to 1973, the Norwegians alone caught 52,000 animals and about 2,000 animals per year, on average, over the period from 1969 to 1975. The Japanese and Koreans also hunted the stock heavily, especially in the second half of the century. They caught animals from the North Pacific. Also, the peoples of South Africa and South America hunted the minke whale stocks of the Southern Hemisphere.

The death rate of minke whale in the Southern Hemisphere from natural causes is believed to be 9-10%, which is much higher than for other rorqual whales. Among the most virulent enemies there is the killer whale, which is thought to attack and kill this small rorqual on a large scale. Minke whales constitute about 85% of the killer whale's diet.

The world stock of minke whales is thought to be about 1,000,000 animals: about 750,000 in the Antarctic Ocean and some 180,000 in the North Atlantic (ca. 55,000 of these around Iceland).

where to go

for a whale watching in iceland

The parties listed below offer whale watching trips in Iceland (March 1997). The item numbers refer to the locations marked on the map of Iceland to the right. We advise all those planning to go on a whale watching trip to reserve space well in advance, carry along good, protective outerwear and, of course, remember binoculars along with a video and/or regular camera. Cameras with an 80-200 mm zoom lens have proved best.

1) Norðursigling

P.O. Box 122, 640 Húsavík.
Location: Húsavík harbour.
Árni Sigurbjarnarson.
Tel: 464-2350.
Fax: 464-2351.
E-mail: nsail@est.is
http://www.north-sailing.is

1) Arnar Sigurðsson

Litlagerði 8, 640 Húsavík.
Location: Húsavík harbour.
Arnar Sigurðsson.
Tel: 464-1748 / 854-2948.
Fax: 872-1248.

2) Jöklaferðir hf.

P.O. Box 66, 780 Höfn.
Location: Höfn harbour.
Tryggvi Árnason.
Tel: 478-1000.
Fax: 478-1901.

3) Íslensk hvalaskoðun

Only for groups.
P.O. Box 52, 220 Hafnarfj.
Location: Keflavík harbour.
Tel: 565-5555 / 894-1388.
Fax: 565-4611.

3) HI Ferðaþjónusta

Tunguvegi 12, 260 Njarðvík.
Location: Njarðvík harbour.
Helga Ingimundardóttir.
Tel: 421-3361 / 896-5598.
Fax: 421-3361.

4) Boat trips

Location: Arnarstapi.
Sölvi Konráðsson.
Tel: 435-6783 / 854-2832.
Fax: 435-6795.

5) Eyjaferðir

Stykkishólmi.
Location: Stykkishólmur harbour.
Tel: 438-1450.

6) Húni II

Location: Harbours in Húnaflói.
Þorvaldur Skaptason.
Tel: 555-2758 / 854-1388.

7) Sjóferðir

Ráðhús Dalvíkur, 620 Dalvík.
Location: Dalvík.
Símon Ellertsson.
Tel: 466-3355.
Fax: 466-1661.

7) Níels Jónsson

Aðalgata 15, 621 Dalvík.
Location: Hauganes.
Tel: 466-1690.
Fax: 466- 3245.

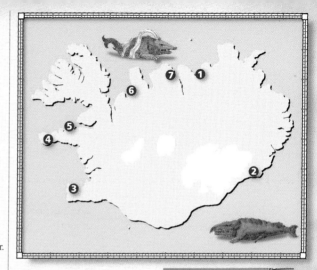

"An adventure of stunning beauty…" Onboard Norðursigling's boat Knörr from Húsavík.

PHOTO: HEIMIR HARÐARSON

KNÖRRINN

*Whale-watching…
…or whales watching
whale watchers?
The pictures were
taken on Skjálfandi
Bay onboard the Knörr,
North Sailing's
whale-watching
boat in Húsavík.*

references

•Árni Einarsson: HVALIR. In: Villt spendýr. Pp. 19-48. Reykjavík: Landvernd, 1980.
•Bjarni Sæmundsson: ÍSLENSK DÝR II. SPENDÝRIN (MAMMALIA ISLANDIÆ). Reykjavík: Bókaverslun Sigfúsar Eymundssonar, 1932.
•Bonner, Nigel: WHALES OF THE WORLD. London: Blandford, 1989.
•Burton, John A. & Bruce Pearson: RARE MAMMALS OF THE WORLD. London: Collins, 1987.
•Carwardine, Mark: WHALES, DOLPHINS & PORPOISES. London: Dorling Kindersley, 1995.
•Christensen, Ivar: HVALENE. In: Norges dyr, Pattedyrene 2. Pp. 34-74. Osló: J. W. Cappelens Forlag AS, 1990.
•Commission of the European Communities: MULTILINGUAL ILLUSTRATED DICTIONARY OF AQUATIC ANIMALS AND PLANTS. Brussels, Luxembourg: Fishing News Books, 1993.
•Darling, James D. et al.: WHALES, DOLPHINS AND PORPOISES. National Geographic Society. 1995.
•Ellis, Richard: MONSTERS OF THE SEA. New York, London, Toronto, Sydney, Auckland: Doubleday, 1996.
•Evans, Peter G. H.: THE NATURAL HISTORY OF WHALES AND DOLPHINS. London: Christopher Helm, 1990.
•Gaskin, D. E.: WHALES, DOLPHINS AND SEALS: WITH SPECIAL REFERENCE TO THE NEW ZEALAND REGION. London: Heinemann, 1972.
•Gozmány, László: VOCABULARIUM NOMINUM ANIMALIUM EUROPAE SEPTEM LINGUIS REDACTUM. I-II. Budapest: Akadémiai Kiadó, 1979.
•Hershkovitz, Philip: CATALOG OF LIVING WHALES. Bulletin of the U.S. National Museum, no. 246. Washington: Smithsonian Institution. 1966.
•Heuvelmans, Bernard: IN THE WAKE OF THE SEA-SERPENTS. London: Rupert Hart-Davis, 1968.
•Jóhann. Sigurjónsson: HVALIR. In: Nytjastofnar sjávar og umhverfisþættir 1991. Hafrannsóknastofnun Fjölrit nr. 25. Reykjavík: Hafrannsóknastofnun, 1991.
•Jóhann Sigurjónsson: HVALRANNSÓKNIR VIÐ ÍSLAND. In: Villt íslensk spendýr. Pp. 103-146. Reykjavík: Hið íslenska í náttúrufræðifélag/Landvernd, 1993.
•Jón Guðmundsson: EIN STUTT UNDIRRIETTING UM ÍSLANDS ADSKILJANLEGAR NÁTTÚRUR. In: Islandica, XV. Ithaca, New York: Cornell University Library, 1924.
•KONUNGS SKUGGSJÁ, SPECULUM REGALE. Magnús Már Lárusson bjó til prentunar. Reykjavík: Leiftur, [no year].
•Krane, Willibald: FISH: FIVE-LANGUAGE DICTIONARY OF FISH, CRUSTACEANS AND MOLLUSCS. Hamburg: Behr, 1986.
•Leatherwood, Stephen & Randall R. Reeves: THE SIERRA CLUB HANDBOOK OF WHALES AND DOLPHINS. San Francisco: Sierra Club Books,1983.

•Lúðvik Kristjánsson: HVALUR. In: Íslenzkir sjávarhættir, V. Pp. 25-90. Reykjavík: Bókaútgáfa Menningarsjóðs, 1986.
•Macdonald, David (ed.): WHALES AND DOLPHINS. In: The Encyclopaedia of Mammals: 1. Pp. 162-237. London: Georg Allen & Unwin, 1984.
•Macdonald, David & Priscilla Barrett: MAMMALS OF BRITAIN AND EUROPE. Somerset: Collins, 1995.
•Martin, Anthony R. (ed.): WHALES AND DOLPHINS. London, New York: Salamander Books Ltd., 1990.
•Negedly, Robert: ELSEVIER'S DICTIONARY OF FISHERY, PROCESSING, FISH AND SHELLFISH NAMES OF THE WORLD IN FIVE LANGUAGES. Amsterdam, New York, Tokyo, Oxford: Elsevier, 1990.
•Organisation for economic co-operation and development: MULTILINGUAL DICTIONARY OF FISH AND FISH PRODUCTS. Paris: Fishing News Books, 1990.
•Óskar Ingimarsson & Þorsteinn Thorarensen: HVALIR. In: Spendýr. Undraveröld dýranna, 12. Icelandic translation of Grande enciclopedia illustrata degli animali. Pp. 141-180. Reykjavík: Fjölvaútgáfan/Veröld, 1988.
•Ridgway, Sam H. (ed.): HANDBOOK OF MARINE MAMMALS. Vol. 3. Sirenians and baleen whales. San Diego: Academic Press Limited, 1985.
•Ridgway, Sam H. & Richard J. Harrison (ed.): HANDBOOK OF MARINE MAMMALS. Vol. 4. River dolphins and the larger toothed whales. San Diego: Academic Press Limited, 1989.
•Ridgway, Sam H. & Richard J. Harrison (ed.): HANDBOOK OF MARINE MAMMALS. Vol. 5. The first book of dolphins. San Diego: Academic Press Limited, 1994.
•Thomas, Lars: DYRENE, DER IKKE BURDE EKSISTERE. In: Tidsskriftet Antropologi, nr. 33. Pp. 37-49. København: Foreningen Stofskifte, 1996.
•Tønnessen, J. N. & Johnsen, A. O.: THE HISTORY OF MODERN WHALING. London: C. Hurst & Company / Canberra: Australian National University Press, 1982.
•Vibe, Christian: PATTEDYR (MAMMALIA). In: Grønlands fauna. Opp. 363-459. København: Gyldendal, 1990.
•Watson, Lyall: WHALES OF THE WORLD. London, Melbourne, Sydney, Auckland, Johannesburg: Hutchinson, 1985.
•Þorvaldur Gunnlaugsson: HVALATALNINGAR. In: Villt íslensk spendýr. Pp. 160-174. Reykjavík: Hið íslenska náttúrufræðifélag/Landvernd, 1993.

The authors furthermore made use of information from a number of other books and magazines, as well as oral sources.

sincere gratitude to:

The Ministry for the Environment,
Mark Carwardine,
Jóhann Páll Valdimarsson,
Ólöf Eldjárn,
and all others who made this
book possible.